FAST ▶▶ FORWARD

LEVEL 5 TO LEVEL 6

SUE HACKMAN

Hodder & Stoughton

A MEMBER OF THE HODDER HEADLINE GROUP

Contents

The contents chart below reflects the different ways that this book can be used. Firstly, by looking down each column, you can see what each unit consists of and work your way through the book accordingly. Secondly, by looking across each row, you are able to follow each strand for particular emphasis in that area, concentrating on one of the strands and using the relevant parts of each unit. For example, to work on 'Improving Sentences' follow the row across and simply use the page references to go to the specific sections of each unit.

This book offers an intensive programme for raising pupils from Level 5 to Level 6 in English. The content is broadly applicable to pupils in Key Stage 3, but would not be lost on able pupils in Year 6 preparing for the extension paper in English.

It is built directly around the critical features of Level 6 and the feedback from QCA about those pupils who strive but fail to reach it. The purpose of the book is to raise the game of pupils who have reached a plateau at Level 5. It is deliberately direct, focused and helpful about doing well in examination conditions.

There may well be pupils who are currently at Level 4 but looking for a Level 5 result in the KS3 tests who would find useful advice about examination skills in The Art of Analysis and Reading Between the Lines strands.

What is involved in getting a Level 6?

The move from Level 5 to 6 is the one from competence to control. Working at Level 5, the pupil is already a 'good' reader and writer, though there may be weak spots in performance.

To move to Level 6, the pupil must –

In reading:

- detect layers of meaning
- comment on significance and effect
- give a full personal response and justify it
- summarise information culled from different sources.

In writing:

- engage and hold the reader's attention

- be versatile in expression and ambitious in the use of sentence structure
- be confident in punctuation and spelling, even in more complex cases.

There are two key tasks facing pupils at Level 5. One is to achieve control over their own language at word, sentence and text level so that they are consciously managing their own reading and writing processes. The other is to sweep up outstanding weaknesses. It is, after all, possible to have achieved Level 5 whilst still harbouring persistent weaknesses. It is hardly likely that they will go away without direct attention at this stage. Common weaknesses at Level 5 include:

- Spelling words in which there are tricky choices to be made, particularly between different ways of spelling the same sound, e.g. 'LE' or 'EL' at the end of a word.
- Uncertain use of the comma for breaking up longer sentences.
- Writing stories that run out of steam half-way through.
- Unfocused answers in examination conditions.
- Fear of non-fiction.

This book has been constructed around the three bullet lists above. It is a teaching book, because at this age and level, pupils are well aware of their own weaknesses (loathe as they are to discuss them) and are not to be patronised with phoney activities and the depressing prospect of the long slow haul to literacy. Why not make life easier by telling them now what they need to know so that they can get on trying and applying it?

Moving from Level 5 to Level 6 in reading

A reader at Level 5 has sound understanding and has begun to read between the lines. Typically, he or she can pick out main points, express a view and back it up with evidence. Given a research task, this reader could find and collate information. In other words, the reader has acquired a set of reading tools and behaviours and can use them.

Typically, a Level 5 pupil will have good understanding but thinner interpretation, make three good points but miss their deeper significance, have a sense of the overarching meaning but not fully articulate it. You can see that one of the dangers at Level 5 is that pupils who do as the teacher tells them sometimes hit a ceiling here. They go through the right routines, they perform the correct behaviours, but they lack the cohesion and penetration that comes from independent critical thinking.

Under-taught pupils at Level 5 will be in a worse situation, because they will sense all these things but lack the tools and routines to articulate them. Of these pupils, teachers will say that they are wonderful in discussion but disappointing on the page. They will make big strong points then fail to back them up or develop them. It is as though meaning is obvious to them and they don't know what else to do but state it. A lot of boys do this. There will be telling moments of clarity and brilliance which signal that they could be doing so much better. It is the first and clearest of this book's aims to provide these tools and routines.

The difference between Level 5 and Level 6 is that the reader is more critical and comprehensive in their response. Small features at word level ring bells and make links with text level meanings. The text is perceived as a whole, with its different features working together. The Level 6 reader can hear the orchestra play but can at the same time appreciate the particular contribution of the cello.

This reader is an independent and perceptive reader. Where at Level 5 they collated information, now they synthesise it. Where they used inference at Level 5 they now see different layers of meaning. Where they identified key features, they now see significance. They appreciate so much more. It is around this raised appreciation that the reading sections of this book are organised.

Moving from Level 5 to Level 6 in writing

Level 5 is a formidable level descriptor characterised by writing which is 'varied', 'interesting', 'clear', 'imaginative' and 'precise', but curiously deflated by cautious descriptions at the end of it which refer to basic skills which are only 'usually' right.

In reality, we can say that pupils at Level 5 are pretty good writers already. Many of them have got where they are by reading a lot. They are sure-footed with familiar styles and tasks, because they know how they should sound and look, and they can also make a business-like sentence. The Level 5 writer is leaning on the familiar, is confident with the commonplace and (as is the case with reading), is in danger of sitting on a plateau hoping that experience alone will raise their game.

The writer more than the reader may have come through the system with outstanding weaknesses, particularly in spelling. Vowel choices can be poor, especially if the vowel is unstressed. Pupils with good visual memories will have resolved this problem, but others will still be troubled by alternative ways of making the same sound.

15% of all spelling errors in the Key Stage 3 test are homophone errors.

Similarly, as the pupil strives to create more elaborate sentences, the demands on punctuation increase. You have to be confident with internal sentence punctuation to get to Level 6. If you can't use the comma and the semi-colon to partition clauses, then you will be constrained in expression and the formation of complex thought. It is not unusual to find pupils stuck on Level 5 because they employ avoidance strategies, keeping to short sentences and unambitious vocabulary because they are afraid of making mistakes with complex spelling and sentence grammar.

The Level 6 descriptor does not give much away. If anything, it is rather less robust in its expectations than Level 5. Writing 'often' engages the reader and shows 'some' adaptation, and spelling is 'generally' accurate, punctuation 'usually' correct. It paints an image of a writer whose errors are gradually dying away (how?) and at the same time developing ever more dazzling skills for impressing the reader: 'engages and sustains the reader's attention', 'uses a range of sentence structures and varied vocabulary to create effects'. A glance at Level 7 reveals that the same pupil has acquired the gloss of self-assurance: 'confident', 'developed', 'coherent'.

The most obvious task for writers seeking Level 6 is to secure absolute confidence in the management of sentences and expression, so that they can lift themselves from safe competence to writerly performance. It is for many the move from mimicking styles to finding one's own. Much the same is true of composition: this writer understands that the story is not an end in itself but a form of play between writer and reader: the process is everything, and the skill lies in the telling.

About the structure of this book

This book is divided into ten units, which take a minimum of 3 hours each to deliver. Each unit is divided into 6 sections, which run through the book. The units which require writing – units 5 and 6 in particular – would benefit from more time and would comfortably occupy a whole lesson if the teacher took the opportunity to share and discuss answers. It would be possible to pursue one strand intensively over a short period, as long as one took care to follow it through in ordinary lessons thereafter, ensuring the lessons are applied.

1 Word Builder

This section contains two parts:

- Spelling – which deals with some of the more difficult spelling choices.

- Vocabulary – which deals with strategies for getting at meaning and expanding vocabulary.

2 Reading Between the Lines

This section models and applies strategies for reaching the different layers of meaning in text. It moves from inference and deduction to symbolic meaning. The activities lend themselves to group or class work so that different perspectives are pooled and compared. Hearing others think aloud models the internal processes of effective readers, sifting their impressions and monitoring meaning.

3 Improving Sentences

This is a critical section because it is the most common factor holding back pupils from Level 6. Its purpose is to offer immediate and practical ideas for developing more sophisticated sentences. The overarching aim is to create more versatile writing and mature expression. If you have not ventured here before, you could add the parallel strand in the sister book *Fast Forward: Level 4 to Level 5* which offers 'safe' activities based around interesting sentences lifted from texts.

The best way to teach this unit is to lead from the front, allowing pupils in pairs to devise sentences in the way suggested. The value you can add to the book is in discussing the various merits of the proffered ideas. This models for pupils the internal rehearsal, which goes on inside the head of good writers, and provides them with a way of inspecting their own sentences. Writing is, after all, the supreme medium for self-inspection. Unlike spoken language it waits on the page and allows for revision.

 ## 4 Narrative Style

This is a writing section targeted at pupils whose stories wilt after a strong opening, or whose style lacks variety. Each session explains, exemplifies and practises techniques for improving story design and development. Many of the insights will inform reading.

 ## 5 The Art of Analysis

This section is included for two reasons. One is to help pupils to adopt a more critical and analytical approach to texts. The second is to help them do their best in test conditions by explaining and justifying their views. This section shows them how to find and present their insights.

 ## 6 Managing Information

This section moves pupils on from collating to synthesising information. Unlike the other strands, it forms a continuous exercise, each one building and developing the skills from the last unit. Each unit gives advice and raw material from which new texts must be created. Strategies for approaching the tasks are explained and supported.

There are two further things to say about the use of this book. The first is that no book can do the job on its own. The book will benefit from active teaching which develops learning by discussing the pupils' own suggestions. This interplay between first attempts and self-improvement is a realm that only teachers tread and no textbook can go. No textbook or computer program, however 'interactive', can give the subtlety and precision of feedback that a teacher can provide. The second thing to say is not to linger over the activities. Push hard and fast and expect pupils to learn on the wing. The skills here are well within the grasp of a pupil who is clever enough to have made Level 5. They already have the seeds of self-learning and ambition. Don't bore them. Expect quick progress. Aim high and they will too.

Sue Hackman

September 2000

FAST ▶▶
FORWARD
▶▶▶▶▶

SPELLING:
Hard-to-hear vowels

Here is a list of words that are often misspelt by just one letter. Read them aloud and work out why the misspelt letters are hard to hear.

In twos or threes, discuss:

● Which letter is missing in each case.

● Why it is often misspelt.

● If you don't know the correct letter, how you could work it out.

● If you can't work it out, how you can learn it once you do know.

defin_te	temp_rature
sep_rate	p_rsue
mir_cle	compr_mise
veg_table	orig_nal
coll_ge	cons_nant
ben_fit	desp_rate
marg_rine	marr_age
contr_versial	oct_gon

Check your answers on page 130.

To work it out:

● **Think of family words,** e.g. oct_gonal. Sometimes you can hear the sound more clearly in that word, or you will know that spelling.

● **Think of the meaning.** Does it contain a word or a word root you know? (e.g. the root of cons_nant means 'sound' and other words use it.)

● **Find other words within the word,** e.g. orig_nal contains a drink.

To learn a spelling

1 Think of three ways of learning to see the tricky letter in a word.
2 Think of at least two ways to remember a word by saying rather than seeing it.

VOCABULARY: Working it out

In twos or threes discuss:

● The possible meanings of the boldface words.

● If you don't know the meaning, how you could work it out without a dictionary.

> The waiter had a **sycophantic** manner. He clearly expected a huge tip.

> Rivals fans arrived, their **raucous** laughter and **intimidating** behaviour upsetting the local residents.

> The gently **undulating** countryside was **traversed** by a slowly **meandering** river.

> **Matricide** is a rare crime, but more than ten cases came to court last year.

> The night was warm and calm. We dozed in our chairs, and the **mellifluous** music of the flute floated over the water.

> **Antipathy** grew between the two girls.

To work it out:

● Do you recognise parts of the word, e.g. anti? Try linking the unknown word with a known word to find the meaning they have in common.

● Use the context to work out what meanings are probable.

● Are there clues in the sound of the word? Many words are onomatopoeic: they sound like the thing they describe, e.g. mellifluous, meandering.

Activity

● Rewrite the sentences above substituting alternative words which you think mean the same.

● Look up the words in a dictionary to find out how close you were to understanding them.

READING BETWEEN THE LINES: Making deductions

Good readers pick up hints from the writer and make their own deductions. But how do they do that?

In this passage, the writer describes an old lady called Mrs Pratchett. He doesn't actually tell the reader that he hates her, although this is made clear by the language that he uses to describe her.

> Her name was Mrs Pratchett. She was a small skinny old hag with a moustache on her upper lip and a mouth as sour as a green gooseberry. She never smiled. She never welcomed us when we went in, and the only times she spoke were when she said things like, "I'm watchin' you so keep yer thievin' fingers off them chocolates!". Or "I don't want you in 'ere just to look around! Either you forks out or you gets out!".

The reader can deduce that the writer does not like Mrs Pratchett.

He describes her appearance in an uncomplimentary way:

- as a hag

- he says she has a moustache (suggests she is masculine)

- use of negative adjectives: small, skinny, old

- "a mouth as sour as a green gooseberry".

He describes her behaviour in an uncomplimentary way:

- "She never smiled."

- "She never welcomed us."

- the way he repeats the word 'never'.

He presents her speech in an uncomplimentary way:

- rude to customers

- sneering tone

- concerned only with money.

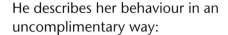

Now read the next paragraph and pick out the ways in which the writer implies his dislike for Mrs Pratchett.

But by far the most loathsome thing about Mrs Pratchett was the filth that clung around her. Her apron was grey and greasy. Her blouse had bits of breakfast all over it, toast-crumbs and tea stains and splotches of dried egg-yolk. It was her hands, however, that disturbed us most. They were disgusting. They were black with dirt and grime. They looked as though they had been putting lumps of coal on the fire all day long. And do not forget please that it was these very hands and fingers that she plunged into the sweet-jars when we asked for a pennyworth of Treacle Toffee or Wine Gums or Nut Clusters or whatever.

There were precious few health laws in those days, and nobody, least of all Mrs Pratchett, ever thought of using a little shovel for getting out the sweets as they do today. The mere sight of her grimy right hand with its black fingernails digging an ounce of Chocolate Fudge out of a jar would have caused a starving tramp to go running from the shop. But not us. Sweets were our life-blood. We would have put up with far worse than that to get them. So we simply stood and watched in sullen silence while this disgusting old woman stirred around inside the jars with her foul fingers.

From *Boy* by Roald Dahl

When you have done this, work out how many times the writer **tells us** what to think about Mrs Pratchett, for example:

'They were disgusting'

and how many times the writer **shows us** about Mrs Pratchett, for example:

'foul fingers'

'grimy right hand'.

Activity

- Now write a brief paragraph of your own describing an unpleasant person. Concentrate on **showing** rather than **telling**, so that your reader has to 'read between the lines'. Use some of the devices you have noted in this unit.

IMPROVING SENTENCES:
Pronouns

Explanation

The word pronoun comes from Latin and means 'in place of a noun'.

The pronouns are:

I	Me	Mine
You	You	Yours
He	Him	His
She	Her	Hers
It	It	Its
We	Us	Ours
They	Them	Theirs

You use the words on the left if they are the ones doing the action, and the words in the middle if they are 'done to'.

> e.g. He called to her.
>
> She replied to him.

Why would you use the words on the right?

Pronouns are important because:

● they remind you who is doing what

● they are quicker and less clumsy than saying the name over and over again

● they link actions and sentences together.

Examples

> There was a knock at the door and Saunders entered. He was youngish, perhaps not more than thirty or so, but sunken-eyed and haggard. With him as their guide they returned to ground level.

Activity

• Spot the pronouns (there are four).

• Who do the pronouns refer to?

• How close to the original noun does a pronoun have to be, to make sense? How long can you go on saying *he* or *they* before you have to say the name again?

• If pronouns had not been used in this passage, which words would you have to substitute? Would this have improved the passage, or not?

Problems of ambiguity

This passage is about two unsuccessful burglars:

> Wallace was not scared of dogs but his timid friend Burton had one fierce hope: that Mickey the Doberman would not wake. But he lay between Wallace and Burton and the door. With infinite care he lifted his left foot, but at that moment he gave him a shove in the back that sent him sprawling right on top of him. He opened an angry eye. At which point he emitted a sound like an engine whirring. Wallace and Burton ran.

From *Sacred Hunger* by Barry Unsworth

- What is wrong with the use of pronouns in this passage?

- How would you improve it? Make three suggestions.

- Where and when is it useful to say the noun again?

- This passage is from an adventure story in which a man is escaping in a boat:

> There was nothing else to do but to swim after him and take my luck with the sharks. So I opened <u>my clasp-knife</u> and put it in my mouth, and took off my clothes and waded in. As soon as I was in the water I lost sight of <u>the canoe</u>, but I aimed, as I judged, to head it off. I hoped <u>the man</u> in it was too bad to navigate it, and that it would keep from drifting in the same direction.

From *Aepyornis Island* by H G Wells

Find the word 'it', which is used five times. Who or what does 'it' refer to on each occasion and how do you know?

Find the underlined phrases and discuss why, in each case, the writer chose to name the noun instead of using a pronoun.

Investigation

Activity

- Find 100 words in the middle of a novel. Pick out all the pronouns.
- Convert all the nouns to pronouns, then read the passage aloud. Discuss the effect.
- Convert all the pronouns to nouns, then read the passage aloud. Discuss the effect.
- Write a guideline of advice about when to use a noun and when to use a pronoun.

Look at your last substantial piece of writing. Check your own use of pronouns.

NARRATIVE STYLE:
Narrative hooks

Writers aim to capture the attention of readers and keep them hooked so that they turn over the next page, and the next. The urge to know what happens next is one of the main pleasures of reading. How do writers keep you 'hooked'?

There are several ways of keeping readers hooked, for example:

- Setting a challenge (e.g. who did this?).

- Keeping them guessing (e.g. it wasn't who you thought it was).

- Describing a curious, intriguing or unusual situation that needs explanation (e.g. the clock was striking thirteen).

- Making them wonder (e.g. why on earth did he do that?).

- Making them care passionately about a character's fate (e.g. will they make it?).

- Leaving things left unsaid so you wonder what is being kept from you (e.g. did he find the letter?).

- Dropping clues for the reader to look for (e.g. only two people had that key).

- Making them wait for answers.

- Cliffhanger endings to chapters.

- Making the reader expect something to happen which the characters don't know about.

Find examples of narrative hooks in the opening of *Brighton Rock* by Graham Greene and decide what kind of hooks they are.

Hale knew, before he had been in Brighton three hours, that they meant to murder him. With his inky fingers and his bitten nails, his manner cynical and nervous, anybody could tell he didn't belong – belong to the early summer sun, the cool Whitsun wind off the sea, the holiday crowd. They came in by train from Victoria every five minutes, rocked down Queen's Road standing on the tops of the little local trams, stepped off in bewildered multitudes into fresh and glittering air: the new silver paint sparkled on the piers, the cream houses ran away into the west like a pale Victorian water-colour; a race in miniature motors, a band playing, flower gardens in bloom below the front, an aeroplane advertising something for the health in pale vanishing clouds across the sky.

It had seemed quite easy to Hale to be lost in Brighton. Fifty thousand people besides himself were down for the day, and for quite a while he gave himself up to the good day, drinking gins and tonics wherever his programme allowed. For he had to stick closely to a programme...

Make a list of questions that the reader would want answering at this point.

e.g. Who are 'they' and why are they trying to murder him?

Here is an incident from George Eliot's *Silas Marner*. Find examples of narrative hooks and decide what kind of hooks they are.

Jem Rodney, the mole-catcher, averred that one evening as he was returning homeward he saw Silas Marner leaning against a stile with a heavy bag on his back, instead of resting the bag on the stile as a man in his senses would have done; and that, on coming up to him, he saw that Marner's eyes were set like a dead man's, and he spoke to him, and shook him, and his limbs were stiff, and his hands clutched the bag as if they'd been made of iron; but just as he had made up his mind that the weaver was dead, he came all right again, like, as you might say, in the winking of an eye, and said 'Good-night', and walked off.

And where did Master Marner get his knowledge of herbs from – and charms too, if he liked to give them away? Jem Rodney's story was no more than what might have been expected by anybody who had seen how Marner had cured Sally Oates, and made her sleep like a baby, when her heart had been beating enough to burst her body, for two months and more, while she had been under the doctor's care. He might cure more folks if he would; but he was worth speaking fair, if it was only to keep him from doing you a mischief.

Try it

Activity

Write a paragraph in which you begin to make your readers curious about the behaviour of your best friend. Don't say what is strange; let your readers work it out for themselves.

Write another paragraph in which an everyday event turns strange and even dangerous. Don't say it is strange and dangerous; let your readers work it out for themselves.

To hook your readers:
- Show rather than tell.
- Drop clues rather than explanations.
- Let the reader do the worrying and guessing.
- Read back your own work as if you were the reader and see if it would keep *you* guessing.

THE ART OF ANALYSIS:
Annotating a text

Test questions often ask you to read and interpret a passage. High marks can be gained by explaining how you arrived at your interpretation. This means picking out the clues in the text. It helps to have a system for doing this.

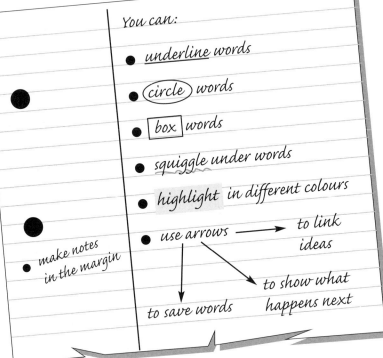

The passages opposite are from *Lord of the Flies* by William Golding. Jack is one of a group of schoolboys stranded on a desert island after a plane crash. In these passages, Jack is hunting a pig.

The question is:

What do you learn about Jack and his surroundings in this passage?

1 **Box** given or factual information about Jack.

2 **Circle** factual information about the surroundings.

3 **Underline** clues, hints and implied information about Jack.

4 **Squiggle** under clues, hints and implied information about the surroundings.

5 Next to the 'clues and hints', write a word or two in the margin to say what it hints at.

6 Join up any circles or boxes that seem to go together and add up to the same thing. Make a note of what it is in the margin.

Try to pick out:

- any interesting descriptive words
- comparisons or contrasts
- links or patterns in the language
- unusual images

- words which carry suggested meanings
- anything else you find interesting

An example has been done for you.

creepy

athletic

Jack was bent double. He was down like a sprinter, his nose only a few inches from the humid earth. The tree trunks and the creepers that festooned them lost themselves in a green dusk thirty feet above him; and all about was the undergrowth. There was only the faintest indication of a trail here; a cracked twig and what might be the impression of a hoof. He lowered his chin and spoke to the traces as though he would like them to speak to him. Then, dog-like, uncomfortable on all fours yet unheeding his discomfort, he stole forward five yards and stopped. Here was a loop of creeper with a tendril pendant from a node. The tendril was polished on the underside; pigs passed through the loop, brushed it with their bristly hide.

intelligent

sharp senses

intense, involved

rainforest

tough

stealthy

logical

animal /
human
habitation

Here is another passage about the same boy. This time, the question is:

What is Jack's state of mind?

Copy and annotate it.

At length he let out his breath in a long sigh and opened his eyes. They were bright blue, eyes that in this frustration seemed bolting and nearly mad. He passed his tongue across dry lips and scanned the uncommunicative forest. Then again he stole forward and cast this way and that over the ground.

The silence of the forest was more oppressive than the heat, and at this hour of the day there was not even the whine of insects. Only when Jack himself roused a gaudy bird from a primitive nest of sticks was the silence shattered and echoes set ringing by a harsh cry that seemed to come out of the abyss of ages. Jack himself shrank at this cry with a hiss of indrawn breath; and for a minute became less a hunter than a furtive thing, ape-like among the tangle of trees.

MANAGING INFORMATION:
Organising your facts

Freelance reporter Carol faces a problem as she takes notes from the file: how best to record the information. The problem is that it comes in such different forms. How can she make it manageable? Should she use a flowchart, a spider diagram, a timeline, a brainstorming mind map, a database or some other way of assembling the information?

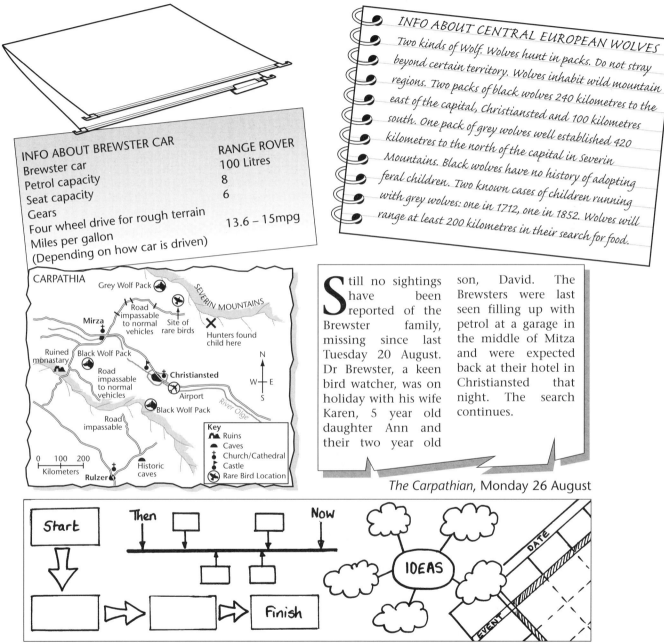

INFO ABOUT CENTRAL EUROPEAN WOLVES
Two kinds of Wolf. Wolves hunt in packs. Do not stray beyond certain territory. Wolves inhabit wild mountain regions. Two packs of black wolves 240 kilometres to the east of the capital, Christiansted and 100 kilometres south. One pack of grey wolves well established 420 kilometres to the north of the capital in Severin Mountains. Black wolves have no history of adopting feral children. Two known cases of children running with grey wolves: one in 1712, one in 1852. Wolves will range at least 200 kilometres in their search for food.

INFO ABOUT BREWSTER CAR	RANGE ROVER
Brewster car	100 Litres
Petrol capacity	8
Seat capacity	6
Gears	
Four wheel drive for rough terrain	13.6 – 15mpg
Miles per gallon	
(Depending on how car is driven)	

CARPATHIA

Grey Wolf Pack
SEVERIN MOUNTAINS
Road impassable to normal vehicles
Mirza
Site of rare birds
Hunters found child here
Ruined monastary
Black Wolf Pack
Road impassable to normal vehicles
Christiansted
Airport
River Olge
Black Wolf Pack
Road impassable

N
W — E
S

0 100 200
Kilometers
Rulzer
Historic caves

Key
🏔 Ruins
🕳 Caves
⛪ Church/Cathedral
🏰 Castle
✈ Rare Bird Location

Still no sightings have been reported of the Brewster family, missing since last Tuesday 20 August. Dr Brewster, a keen bird watcher, was on holiday with his wife Karen, 5 year old daughter Ann and their two year old son, David. The Brewsters were last seen filling up with petrol at a garage in the middle of Mitza and were expected back at their hotel in Christiansted that night. The search continues.

The Carpathian, Monday 26 August

Start
Then
Now
Finish
IDEAS
DATE
EVENT

Spend a few minutes trying out different methods of making notes about the information provided and then discuss:

● Which you found easiest/hardest and why.

● What gets put in and left out of each one.

● What works best when the information is so varied.

● The benefits of diagrams over written prose for taking notes.

Story to be continued in the next unit …

SPELLING:
More letters than sounds

Explanation

Most sounds in words are represented by one letter. For example, there are three sounds represented by three letters in the words PIG.

Some sounds are represented by two or more letters such as 'SH' or 'AY' or 'EAU'. For example, there are three sounds in the word SHOOT, but they are represented by five letters.

Many letters can make more than one sound, e.g. HOW and SHOW.

Activity

How many sounds are there in these words?

FOX	FISH
DUCK	RABBIT
COW	SNAKE

Check your answers on page 130.

Make a list of single sounds made by more than one letter, e.g. 'SH', 'PH', 'CK'. Underline the ones which can make more than one sound, e.g. 'OW'. These are the hardest.

Spelling errors often happen if they contain an unusual number of letters with alternative ways of sounding out.

Activity: 'GH' words

How many words can you find ending in the cluster 'OUGH'?
For example, rough, plough.
Group them together by rhyme.
Next, brainstorm words containing the cluster 'OUGHT'.
What sound do they make?
Apart from LAUGH can you find any other words using 'AUGH' at the beginning or the end?
Work out a rule for deciding between 'OUGHT' and 'AUGHT'.
List and generalise about words beginning with GH.

VOCABULARY:
Classical suffixes

Some suffixes have distinct meanings, and can be traced back to Latin or Greek words. For example, there are several words ending in 'OLOGY'. They are all nouns which mean the science or study of something; e.g. biology = the study of living things.

Activity

Working in twos or threes, match these OLOGY words with their definitions:

ecology	the study of machines
criminology	the study of the earth's structure
meteorology	the study of religion
astrology	the study of the development of words
geology	the study of birds
technology	the study of human behaviour
ornithology	the study of the atmosphere
psychology	the study of the environment
theology	the study of crime
etymology	the study of the possible effects of stars and planets

Check your answers on page 130.
Can you add any others?

Think of words using the following classical suffixes and work out the meaning of the suffix:

–ling	–orium
–ism	–graphy
–archy	–ette

Look closely at the prefix in front of 'OLOGY', and think of other words that use it. Work out the meaning they have in common, e.g. astrology, astronomy, astronaut.

Transforming endings

What endings would you use to:

Describe a person who specialised in each study? (Only one word is an exception – which one is it?)

Transform each word into an adjective?

Transform each word into an adverb?

Check your answers on page 130.

READING BETWEEN THE LINES: Using empathy

Empathy is when we put ourselves in someone else's shoes so we know how they feel.

Buddy is thirteen and his mum has left home. In this passage, she visits him for the first time in six months.

> He didn't know what to do or say. He hadn't seen her for nearly six months – was he still allowed to hug her like the old days? He thought of shaking hands but that was ridiculous. He leaned against the door frame and swung the door wider so that she could come in, but she shook her head and glanced down the road as if she wanted to go. His heart sank. His mum wasn't coming home; she still hated him for stealing. She turned to him but he looked at the ground and began playing with the catch on the door.

 ## Activity

Discuss what feelings you have for Buddy in this passage.
Surprisingly, the story is not told in the first person (I) but in the third person (he), so how are you made to feel for Buddy?

1 The events are described through his eyes, so we tend to see things from his point of view.

  For example 'He hadn't seen her for six months'.

2 We are allowed to hear his thoughts and feelings

  For example 'His heart sank'.

3 We know from experience that his actions mean he is unhappy.

  For example 'He looked at the ground'.

  Find other details which make sure we see events from Buddy's point of view. Find at least two to go under each heading.

Now read on.

"You don't seem very pleased to see me."

Her voice was accusing, almost angry.

He shrugged and flicked the catch a couple of times to cover up the silence.

"I'd better go, then."

"You can come in if you want." He tried to make it sound friendly but it came out as a mumble.

"No, I'd better go."

Tears began to well up in his eyes and he pressed his thumb hard against the sharp edge of the catch to hurt himself.

"You're all right, are you?"

He nodded and clenched his teeth tightly to stop a tear from sliding out of his eye.

"Why are you all in the dark?"

He turned and looked into the house, pretending that he hadn't noticed that the lights were off.

"I thought you were someone else," he said, keeping his face turned away.

"What?"

He repeated it, louder.

"Oh. You're not in trouble, are you?"

He shook his head and the first tear splashed against his nose as he did so.

"Sure?"

He nodded and kept staring towards the kitchen until he heard her shoes scrape on the doorstep as she started to walk away. He listened as her footsteps faded away, then closed the door and sat down on the bottom step of the stairs. When he leaned forward, the tears ran down his nose and splattered on to his shoes.

He rubbed his eyes fiercely with the sleeve of his pullover, glad that the rough texture made his skin sore. Whenever he started crying he found himself wishing that someone could see him. Like now – he wanted his mum to see and feel sorry for him. Not even his tears were real.

From *Buddy* by Nigel Hinton

Activity

- Go through each of the underlined sections and work out what Buddy is feeling and why. For example:

  'He shrugged and flicked the catch a couple of times to cover the silence' tells us that Buddy is feeling awkward and nervous. Perhaps he is upset that she left him, and thinks she should make the first move.

- Finally, choose a short section of this passage and read it aloud, converting it into the first person, making Buddy the storyteller. For example:

  'I rubbed my eyes fiercely with the sleeve of my pullover, glad that the rough texture made my skin sore....'

- Does this help you to empathise more, or less, with the character of Buddy?

IMPROVING SENTENCES:
Colons and semi-colons

Colons

Study these two sentences:

> His theory of running until he reached camp and the boys had one flaw in it: he lacked the endurance.

From *To Build a Fire* by Jack London

> He had only one fault: he was inclined to lose his temper over relatively minor matters.

The punctuation mark is a colon. At either side of the colon is a complete sentence. The writer has joined the two together using a colon, so that the second is decisively balanced off against the first. It is rather like an equal sign (=) in mathematics. The second half tends to be a summary or consequence of the first.

 Activity

Try writing two sentences using a colon, the first declaring that you refuse to do something and the other declaring that you certainly shall do something.

Semi-colons

Read the examples:

> No-one had lived in the house since her death. The doors were broken from the hinges; the window lights were all broken.

From *Death in the Woods* by Sherwood Anderson

> Hagrid had sent him a large tin of treacle fudge, which Harry decided to soften by the fire before eating; Ron had given him a book called Flying with the Cannons, a book of interesting facts about his favourite Quidditch team; and Hermione had bought him a luxury eagle-feather quill.

From *Harry Potter and the Chamber of Secrets* by J.K. Rowling

> She turned the light low, and slipped stealthily over and kneeled by the sack and felt its ridgy hands with her hands, and fondled them lovingly; and there was a gloating light in her poor old eyes.

From *The Man that Corrupted Hadleyburg* by Mark Twain

> She met him in the sombre lane that led to their house, and clung to his arm in silence; she was repentant no doubt, but Temple would not relent; he was mute and tried to shake her off, but she clung on with great tenacity.

From *A Persistent Woman* by Marjorie Bowen

- Try reading the sentences aloud. Many people can hear the change of tone brought about by a semi-colon.

- Find the semi-colons and consider why they are used instead of a full stop or comma.

- The semi-colon is stronger than a comma and softer than a full stop.

- It is used to join clauses or short sentences without having to use a connective such as 'and', 'because' or 'as well as'. The reader is forced to work out the link between the parts for him or herself.

- It feels slightly dramatic because it introduces a short pause into the sentence.

- It implies a very strong link between the parts.

- The first example replaces a conjunction or connecting word. What word could have gone in its place?

- The second example is a list. It is familiar to see commas separating items in a list. What is the advantage of using a semi-colon here?

- The third example uses a semi-colon where a new sentence could easily have been started. What is the advantage of using the semi-colon?

- Try repunctuating the fourth example to omit the semi-colons. Start new sentences or use connecting words, and discuss the effect.

Task

Activity

Find the two places in this passage where a semi-colon could be used:

From the top of the cliff Leanne could see miles out over the glittering sea. On a clear day you could see France. Inevitably her mind would stray to the kinds of journeys she would make and the thousands, if not millions, of people she would meet. Her mother, watching from the bay window of their house, would worry about her dreamy daughter. Leanne, of course, knew her mother was keeping watch but kept stubbornly turned to the vastness of the sea. If she turned back, it would be an acceptance of her mother's narrow vision, a defeat.

NARRATIVE STYLE:
Zoom lens

Explanation

The way sentences are expressed determines how the reader 'sees' what is described. If the writer describes 'a ship in the distance', an image of a ship far away jumps into the reader's mind. If the writer describes 'a ship made of oak, with brass portholes and golden rivets along its bow', the image is not only more detailed but much closer in the mind's eye: close enough to see the rivets.

With each sentence, the reader refocuses on a new subject, perhaps adopting a new perspective. The writer guides the reader's inner eye.

Read this passage and imagine it done by a camera for a film.

> Mildred had an acute face of a powdery paleness, tightened and much marked about the brown eyes by quizzical horizontal lines, as if bound about by fine threads. The white skin of the cheeks by contrast had now a soft old look. The very blue eyes and the mouth were long, amused, often sarcastic. Her hair, a yellowish grey, had a short sensible cut which quite failed to control or even offer suggestions to its natural fluffiness, and her coiffure, never the same from day to day or even hour to hour, had often a positively unkempt appearance; for Mildred was not always impeccably turned out.

From *An Unofficial Rose* by Iris Murdoch

 Activity

Copy the sketch opposite and draw arrows on it to show how your inner eye travelled around Mildred's face. Compare your sketches.

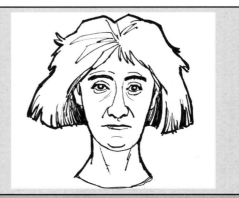

What else did your film camera do? Where did it zoom and change its focus? How far away was it from Mildred?

There are no camera instructions in the text: how, then, is the mind's eye guided by the writer? Look for the topic of each sentence.

Try this exercise again with another paragraph:

Temporary and perilous though men's lives were, the mountains, valleys, and waterfalls were radiant on this fine day with permanence and certainty. The mountain snow sparkled in this sun. Here and there a melting trickle of water twisted down the rocky slopes. Under the snow the pines and firs shone green with their freshness. The breezes which blew from the woods brought the smell of spring into this winter day.

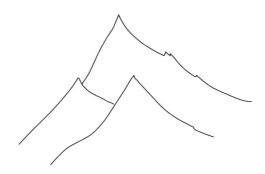

From *The King of the Fields* by Isaac Bashevis Singer

Compare results and discuss how the writer made you visualise this scene.

Try it

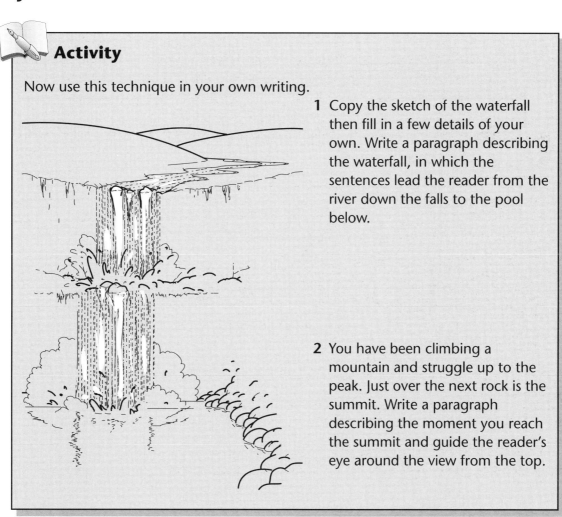

Activity

Now use this technique in your own writing.

1 Copy the sketch of the waterfall then fill in a few details of your own. Write a paragraph describing the waterfall, in which the sentences lead the reader from the river down the falls to the pool below.

2 You have been climbing a mountain and struggle up to the peak. Just over the next rock is the summit. Write a paragraph describing the moment you reach the summit and guide the reader's eye around the view from the top.

THE ART OF ANALYSIS:
How to make and develop a point

In tests, you will be assessed on how well you understand and interpret literature. It is therefore essential that you know how to explain your thinking. First read this poem by James Berry, in which he evokes his earliest memories.

Bits of Early Days

Still a shock to remember, facing
that attacking dog's fangs and eyes
at its gate;
seeing our slug-eating dog come in
the house, mouth gummed up, plastered!

Still a joy to remember, standing
at our palm-fringed beach
watching sunrise streak the sea;
finding a hen's nest in high grass
full of eggs;
riding a horse bareback, galloping.

Still a shock to remember, eating
with fingers and caught oily-handed
by my teacher;
seeing a dog like goat-hide flattened
there in the road.

Still a joy to remember, myself
a small boy milking a cow
in new sunlight;
smelling asafoetida
on a village baby I held;
sucking fresh honey from its comb
just robbed.

Still a shock to remember, watching
weighted kittens tossed in the sea's
white breakers;
seeing our village stream dried up
with rocks exposed
like dry guts and brains.

Still a joy to remember, walking
barefoot on a bed of dry leaves
there in the deep woods;
finding my goat with all of three
new wobbly kids.

Still a shock to remember, facing
that youth-gang attack and all
the needless abuse;
holding my first identity card
stamped "Negro".

Still a joy to remember, walking
fourteen miles from four a.m.
into town market;
surrounded by sounds of church-bell
in sunlight and birdsong.

The question is:

How does the poet bring alive for the reader the memories in each stanza?

The answer for the first stanza is given opposite:

In the first stanza, the poet remembers his terror as a small child when he is confronted by a fierce dog behind a gate, and his revulsion at his own dog after it has eaten slugs. The sudden sharpness of the memory is quickly signalled in the opening words of the stanza: 'Still a shock'. The first dog is made terrifying by the words 'fangs' and 'attacking', and the second dog is made revolting by the words 'slug-eating', 'gummed up' and 'plastered'. The exclamation mark also adds to the sense of suddenness. The language is like speech: 'that dog', as if the poet is saying it just at the moment he remembered it. The overall effect is one of recaptured experience.

The structure of the answer is:

- establishing the key message or impact

- how it is achieved (with evidence for each point made)

- the overall effect

Here are notes for a paragraph about the second stanza. Write up the paragraph, finding evidence to support each item.

> Joy this time – at one with the natural world – sunset at the beach, finding eggs, riding bareback.
>
> Beauty of natural world
>
> In touch with nature
>
> Sense of excitement
>
> Symbols of hope

Next choose one other stanza to write about, keeping to the structure for developing points. Once you are confident with this structure, you can develop it to suit different questions, texts and your own style.

MANAGING INFORMATION:
Identifying patterns

Remind yourself of events so far in Unit 1.

Carol sets about organising her information to convince her editor.

She has to weigh up the different possibilities, comparing the facts to ascertain what is possible and what is likely.

She chooses a grid because with a grid you can compare information.

Activity

Fill in Carol's grid to see how likely it is that the Brewster boy could have ended up with the wolves.

From Mitza	Possible destinations within petrol range	Roads passable/ impassable	Distance from where boy found	Wolf pack in area/ type
EAST				
WEST				
NORTH				
SOUTH				

Carol then writes a note to her editor arguing the strong likelihood that the boy is in fact David Brewster. The note goes through the main factors she considered.

Here are the openings to her first two points.

I think it is very likely that the feral child is David Brewster. The first vital clue is petrol capacity. We know the Brewsters had a Range Rover and …

The second piece of evidence is the road they must have taken on the fateful day. They couldn't have …

Complete these two points and add more, concluding with:

And so it all points to one area and one area only …

Carol faxes the message to her editor when she arrives in Christiansted.

Story to be continued in the next unit …

SPELLING:
Awkward extensions

It's hard to know how to extend a word that ends in a vowel followed by a consonant. Look at the following list of words and what happens to them when 'ED' or 'ING' endings have been added:

target	targeted	targeting
benefit	benefited	benefiting
refer	referred	referring
fulfil	fulfilled	fulfilling
buffet	buffeted	buffeting

Can you work out why some of the words need to double the last letter when 'ED' or 'ING' are added?

HINT

Say the words aloud and try to detect a difference.
Listen where the *stress* falls in the word, e.g. **tar**get.

Activity

- Write the following list then underline the stressed part of each word. Then write the 'ED' and 'ING' endings to them:

Appal

Acquit

Banquet

Batter

Prohibit

Occur

Admit

Check your answers on page 131.

This is only a general rule and there are exceptions. Words ending in 'L' such as TRAVEL often double the 'L' anyway when an ending is added, e.g. travelled, travelling.

VOCABULARY:
Adjectives for the senses

Most adjectives are dedicated to describing what we see. It is harder to find adjectives for the other senses.

Activity

Here are adjectives used to describe different smells. Work out what they mean without using a dictionary and put the words in two columns – one headed 'Good Smells' and one headed 'Bad Smells':

fragrant	malodorous	pungent
acrid	aromatic	scented
reeking	fetid	putrid

HINT

- Some of the 'bad' smells are onomatopoeic and sound sharp and unpleasant.

- Think what the prefix 'mal' (from the French word) means in 'malevolent' and 'malignant'.

- The Latin for 'stinking' is 'fetidus'.

Which of these words would you normally use to describe: herbs and spice; old trainers; burning rubber and mouldy cheese.

Activity

Make a similar list of adjectives to describe tastes and next to each taste, give an example.
Then try a list of adjectives to describe:

- different textures of cloth

- the quality of different liquids on the fingers

- air or climate on the skin, e.g. clammy.

READING BETWEEN THE LINES: Inferring meaning beyond the literal

Literal meaning is stated, but implied meanings can be worked out if one is sensitive to the clues.

Poetry often depends on inference because it has layers of meaning which you have to work out for yourself.

> A poet can sometimes **suggest** meanings by:
>
> - what is left unspoken (gaps in the text which the reader must work out)
>
> - connotation (using words which you associate with other things)
>
> - implication (things that are implied but not stated)
>
> - comparison (using a simile, metaphor or symbol to imply parallels)

Read the following poem by Elizabeth Jennings.

The Smell of Cooking

The smell of cooking rising to my room
Speaks clear of childhood and of many things.
Always, these days, I'm near to tears because
My parents and myself are leaving home.
Even to things that hurt affection clings.

Day after day, I've sorted out my books:
Nothing sensational and yet the whole
Experience is like an open nerve.
My parents and myself exchange cold looks.
Oh, every room is like a brimming bowl.

Where flowers are leaning out and wanting air.
We too. The smell of cooking rises high
But hardly touches me because I know
Three-quarters of me is no longer here.

And yet I love this torn, reproachful sky
And am afraid of where I have to go.

Tasks

1 Write down **all the facts you know** about the person in the poem. For example:

- she is moving house

- she is packing her belongings.

  These are literal things.

2 Now consider what is only **suggested** by the poet. Find in the first two stanzas the suggestions that:

- a particular smell triggers the poet's memory (lines 1–2)

- the poet is upset (line 3)

- the poet is even fond of painful memories (line 5)

- the experience of moving house is painful (line 7–8)

- the poet is upset with her parents (line 9)

3 For each of the five 'suggestions' say whether it works by comparison, implication, connotation or being left unspoken. (See first box opposite).

4 Still looking at what is only suggested, explain what is implied in the three underlined sections.

5 The title has a literal meaning, but the smell itself is not the subject of the poem. Why has it been chosen?

IMPROVING SENTENCES:
Using commas to extend a sentence

Explanation

You know that commas are used to separate items in a list. You also know that commas are used to chunk up sentences to guide the reader through it. When you read aloud, you can sometimes hear a slight pause or shift of tone at the comma. But where exactly do you use a comma to chunk up a sentence?

> They got out, leaving the car by the side of the road, and walked up a grass ride, their feet crunching on the brittle frozen grass.

From *Not that Sort of Girl* by Mary Wesley

Strip back this sentence to its essentials and you are left with 'They got out and walked up the grass ride'. None of the other chunks make sense on their own. They are dependent on this basic sentence for their meaning. Commas are used as buffers between the main clause (the basic sentence) and the other parts.

To write well, you have to extend and elaborate sentences, and to do this you need commas.

Tasks

1 Imitate the sentence 'They got out…' above, changing the content but keeping to the structure and the commas. For example:

They wandered off, leaving the children to play on the swings, and sauntered into the forest, their feet scattering the fallen leaves.

2 Read this sentence:

> The blacksmith lived in the village, a strip of featureless low stone cottages, and rarely visited even the nearby town, where there was at least a pub and a crumbling apology for a cinema.

● Strip back this sentence to its essentials: the bits you can't do without.

● Notice that you could almost use brackets (parentheses) around the remaining parts. This is because they are extras, extensions to the basic sentence.

● Try adding in another extension about the cottages.

● Try adding in another extension about the cinema.

3 Read this sentence:

> The sailor leapt from the deck into the sea without so much as a backward glance.

● Find the main clause. Try to reposition it, remembering to put a comma between it and the rest of the sentence.

● Try placing 'without so much as a backward glance' in the middle of the sentence, again putting commas between it and the rest of the sentence.

● Read aloud the two sentences so that you can hear the shift or pause that has been introduced into your new sentence. If you start with the main clause, you don't need a comma. If you start with a subordinate clause, you do.

HELP

• All sentences have at least one main clause, which is a basic sentence with its own noun and verb, around which subordinate clauses are added as extensions.

• Writing sounds more sophisticated if you sometimes start with a subordinate clause followed by a comma, leading into the main clause.

• It also sounds good to drop extra information into a sentence like an aside, using commas as brackets.

More information can be found in Unit Eight.

HOT TIP

If all this is hard to remember, then try these tips:
• Start with a verb ending in 'ING'

• Start with a verb ending in 'ED'

• Start with an adverb ending 'LY'

• Start with a preposition, e.g. 'OVER'

• Start with anything other than a noun or pronoun!

NARRATIVE STYLE: Cliffhangers

Television has made cliffhanger endings famous. Programmes ending with a cliffhanger make the viewer tune in next time to find out what happens. In literature, cliffhangers can often be found at the end of chapters, sections and scenes for much the same reason.

Example

> For that night (July the twenty-fifth, 1943), as chance would have it, Dad had not been plagued by his usual restlessness. That night he had slept soundly till woken by the dawn, at which he had risen, along with Dick who, never suffering himself from disturbed nights, woke every morning at five-thirty, to depart at six-thirty on his motor-cycle for the outskirts of Lynn, where he worked on a dredger in the Ouse. Only a commotion coming from the front of the cottage, a hoarse shout from Dad, the clanking of someone running over the cat-walk of the sluice, denied me the extra hour's sleep I was allowed as a studious schoolboy (schoolboy then on holiday, and not so exclusively studious) and prevented me from being woken, as I usually was, by the coughings and garglings of Dick's motor-bike.
>
> And when I went into Dick's room to look out over the river, Dad and Dick were standing on the cat-walk, bent forward, eyes lowered, and Dad was prodding something in the water, tentatively, nervously, with a boat-hook, as if he were the keeper of some dangerous but sluggish aquatic animal and were trying to goad it into life.
>
> I flung on my clothes; went downstairs, heart jumping.

From Waterland by Graham Swift

- The ending is clearly a cliffhanger: what do you anticipate?

- But the cliffhanger is not just made in the last line. The writer winds up to it to make it even more tantalising. Find five details which are used by the writer to build the reader's sense that something extraordinary is going to happen.

Here is another cliffhanger from *Wuthering Heights*:

> I wanted something to happen which might have the effect of freeing both Wuthering Heights and the Grange of Mr Heathcliff, quietly, leaving us as we had been prior to his advent. His visits were a continual nightmare to me; and, I suspected, to my master also. His abode at the Heights was an oppression past explaining. I felt that God had forsaken the stray sheep there to its own wicked wanderings, and an evil beast prowled between it and the fold, waiting his time to spring and destroy.

- This is a rather different cliffhanger because there is no event at the end. What, then, makes it feel as if an event is inevitable?

- Identify five details which are used by the writer to build anticipation.

Writers compose cliffhangers so that they:

- stop just before an inevitable, dramatic or gruesome event

- hold the reader in suspense

- make the reader fear the worst

- communicate tension in the vocabulary and pace of the build-up

- make the reader move on to the next part of the story, e.g. the next chapter.

Try it

Here's a plan for a story. Suggest a cliffhanger to end each chapter.

Chapter 1

Hattie comes home from school
Fun evening with father – single parent
Hattie's father announces he is in love again

Chapter 2

Next day at school
Hattie's feelings described
Walk home

Chapter 3

Hattie argues with father
Much misery
Hattie meets Dad's girlfriend

Chapter 4

The three have a meal together
Hattie has mixed feelings
Dad has more news

Chapter 5

Hattie decides to run away from home
Best friend counsels against it
Hattie tries to leave house in middle of night

Activity

Write the final paragraph of any two of the chapters, using some of the techniques studied.

THE ART OF ANALYSIS:
Using quotation to support an answer

Sometimes you need to quote what a writer has written as evidence for a point you are making.

How to quote

- If the quotation is *long*, it might be best to refer to it rather than write it out.

- If it is *a line or a couple of lines long*, and important, you can put a colon to introduce it and then write the quote like this:

    'Here's a quotation. It is indented and has its own space so you can see where my writing stopped and the quotation started. It starts and stops with quotation marks for the same reason.'

- However, if it is *short*, the most common way of quoting is to drop a few well-chosen words into your own sentences. For example 'this short quote' and 'that short quote' or even after a colon: 'a quote at the end'. Notice the quotation marks again.

How do you know when to quote?

Quote if:	Don't quote if:
• The choice of words is particularly important or evocative.	• You can say it quicker and just as easily in your own words.
• You need to say something about the choice and sound of word, or the techniques used.	• The way it is said isn't relevant to your point.
• It's quicker to quote the words than explain them in your own way.	
• If they are especially clever or pithy, or of interest in themselves.	

Opposite is a passage and a student's comment. You will need to consider which parts of the passage you could quote.

The Art of Analysis

Then there was Auntie Gertie – Grandma Barrack's sister. She married a soldier when she was twenty-six. He was killed by an army truck three weeks later and family rumour had it that the grief had sent her mad. Shortly after the accident, she crept into the church where they were married and stole a gold cup from the altar. The scandal circulated the village and the family rocked in shame. My grandma took her sister into her country house and gave her a room of her own. It was small and cold and Auntie Gertie always wore a big teddy bear coat with polished wood buttons. She looked older than she was, probably because she harboured a great inner sorrow which sat in her pale eyes – immovable. Her grey hair hung in a thick plait down her back. She wore dark brown dresses and no embellishments of any kind. Her skin was gently creased. I often wanted to be rude to her, or to laugh at her. But her private smile always outwitted me, so I would leave her sitting there in the old upturned boat which had been made into a shelter at the bottom of the orchard. She always had a wild flower in her hand and never failed to put it in water at the end of the day, and she would rock to and fro, to and fro, but as soon as a bird came down to the ground she would sense it immediately.

From *Instead of Diamonds* by Carla Lane

This is how one student explained how the writer suggests Gertie's grief:

Gertie is still grieving over the death of her new husband, killed three weeks after their marriage. The writer uses dull, drab colours to suggest Gertie's sorrow. 'Her grey hair' and 'dark brown dresses' suggest her depressed state. Her room is 'small and cold', and she herself is 'gently creased' and 'immoveable'. At one point the writer even tells us directly that Gertie is suffering from grief: 'she harboured a great inner sorrow'.

Find examples of:

- Referring to the passage rather than quoting from it.
- Quotation mid-sentence.
- Quotation at the end of a sentence.

- Distinguishing between what is suggested and what is said.

Now write a paragraph which explains how the writer suggests that Gertie is slightly mad. You could make the following points, but you must find the quotations:

> *Family rumour – sent mad by grief for her husband's death.*
>
> *Rash act – stealing cup from church where married.*
>
> *Odd behaviour – rocking, wearing flower, sitting under boat.*
>
> *Cut herself off – stays still all day, uncommunicative.*

- Find quotations to support each point.
- Decide which should be used and which should be told in your own words.
- Play each sentence in your head before you write it down.

MANAGING INFORMATION:
Marshalling different kinds of information

Remind yourself of events so far in previous units.

Carol reviews what she already knows and two new items:

Christiansted Hospital Communiqué

```
Patient's name:   not known
Sex:              male
Age:              not known.
                  Assessed at
                  13
Nationality:      not known
Weight:           8 stone
Height:           5 foot
                  4 inches
Possessions:      bracelet
                  with letters
                  'DRB'

Other details: Patient
admitted on Saturday 11th
August. Has refused all food.
Refuses to wear clothes. Has
not spoken. Stares through
window. Occasionally whines
as if in pain. Has grown
extensive body hair on back
and legs.
```

Family photo

Carol quickly assembles the information that she has got. It isn't much to go on, but Carol knows she can still write a good story.

When you draw together information which is very different in its content, style and presentation, it is probably best to decide in advance the main headings under which you will organise the final piece of writing. You can then fit the information you have under these headings.

Carol decides to organise her material under six headings around the definite facts:

- *Main point of article*
- *Appearance & behaviour of boy*
- *How he was found*
- *About the hospital*
- *The background to the case*
- *His possible future*

Carol will write a paragraph on each point, based on notes under each heading, using the information given so far.

Organising information in an article

The order of information in a newspaper article is rarely linked to the order of events. Rather, it starts with the big news, then picks off the most interesting and newsworthy items in order of fascination. Casual readers can stop reading after they have got the main points, but an eager reader will carry on through the article. The order is devised to fit in with the way people read newspapers, browsing for the main points and what interests them.

1 Assemble notes under each heading.

2 Paragraph starters have been provided for the first two paragraphs of the article. You write the starters for the others. Starter sentences in articles usually contain:

- Fascinating details *to grab the reader's attention* and keep them hooked.

- A pointer to the content of the whole paragraph *to direct the reader's attention.*

- Links to the previous and next points, e.g. 'Now …', 'Later …', *to orientate the reader.*

Main point of article	*Possible links are being drawn between a boy who went missing. . . .*
Appearance & behaviour of boy	*Now he crouches, a pathetically thin. . . .*
How he was found	
About the hospital	
Background to the case	
His possible future	

3 Now write out the article including headline, attention-grabbing first paragraph and the story organised according to your plan.

Story to be continued in the next unit …

SPELLING: Choosing between 'EL', 'LE', 'AL'

Words ending in the 'L' sound are particularly tricky because there are so many ways of spelling that sound. However, there are some general patterns that you should be able to work out.

In twos and threes, search for patterns in the following words that might decide the endings.

'EL'	'LE'	'AL'
parcel	incredible	magical
novel	probable	monumental
cancel	possible	fanatical
model	bottle	physical
morsel	bubble	practical
camel	apple	comical

HINT

Look carefully at the consonants or even the whole words that come immediately before the ending.

Activity

Add 'EL', 'LE', or 'AL' endings to the following words:

cand_ _   parab_ _   fizz_ _
medic_ _   shov_ _   critic_ _
cobb_ _   grov_ _   trav_ _
edib_ _   noticeab_ _   sign_ _   pudd_ _

Check your answers on page 131.

Activity

Make lists of words ending in 'OL', 'UL' or 'IL' and look for patterns.

You will know many words by sight, but if you have trouble remembering, you can often think of similar words with the same endings, e.g. parcel/cancel *but* magical/fanatical. There is a general rule, too: soft 'C' ends in 'EL' and hard 'C' ends in 'AL'.

VOCABULARY:
Fresher words

Do you find yourself using the same inexact words over and over again?

Did you have a <u>nice</u> holiday?

Did you <u>really</u> enjoy yourself?

Are you <u>over the moon</u> about your exam results?

Have you got a <u>bad</u> headache?

Activity

- Think of annoying, over-used words or expressions that you have read or heard people use over and over again.

- Look back at your own work or think of your own speech and make an honest list of your own over-used phrases and words. Brainstorm alternatives to these expressions.

- Many over-used words are used indiscriminately for emphasis, e.g. very, really. Consider alternatives.

- List a range of words or phrases that do the same job but are more subtle about the degree of emphasis, e.g. rather, on the whole.

Fashionable vocabulary

Identify groups of words which come in and out of use as they gain and then lose their freshness, e.g. cool, wicked, funky. What is the current word?

READING BETWEEN THE LINES:
The narrator

A story can be told in a number of different ways. Brainstorm examples of stories that are told:

● in the first person as 'I'

● by two or more different narrators

● by a narrator who tells the story from the outside and seems to know everything that is going on (an omniscient narrator)

● by a narrator who stays close to one character and reveals events that happen to them, rather than knowing about everything

● by a narrator who is a character in the story and unusual in some way.

Compare the narrators in these two passages from *I am the Cheese* by Robert Cormier.

Passage A

> His father's real name was Anthony Delmonte and he had been a reporter in a small town in upstate New York. The name of the town was Blount, population about 30,000. Famous for the high hills veined with granite that loomed above the town. Those hills drew a few Italians across the Atlantic a hundred years ago, men skilled in the uses of marble and granite, among them the grandfather of Adam's father. The Quarries dried up after a while but the Italians remained and became assimilated into the town and state. These were light skinned, blond Italians from Northern Italy. They grew no grapes on terraced slopes. Adam's grandfather was the first of his generation to seek an education; he graduated from law school and was modestly successful, conducting a law office in the heart of Blount.

Passage B

> I pronounce the numbers carefully, exaggerating them, almost a burlesque, but I don't care, I don't want to risk another wrong number. The lights of passing cars flash by, and I realise that I could never have made it this far tonight alone, on the bike.
>
> The phone is ringing, ringing.
>
> I lose count of the rings.
>
> And then! "Hello, hello." That same gruff, impatient voice, not Amy's father, not anybody I know.
>
> "Hello," I say. "Is Amy there?" I feel ridiculous asking the question because I know it's futile.
>
> A pause and then as if he's being very patient: "There's nobody named Amy here. You the kid called earlier? I'm telling you, there's no Amy here."

- What type of narrator is used in each passage?

- Who is the main character in each passage?

- Who is the narrator in each passage?

- How much do you find out about the characters and what is happening to them in each passage?

- What is the effect of the narrative voice on you, the reader, in each passage?

In fact, Adam in Passage A is the narrator of Passage B.

Consider the benefits and limitations, of writing in the first or third person:

	Benefits	Limitations
First person *I*		
Third person *He, she, it, they*		

Collect a few novels or stories you have read recently and try to pinpoint the kind of narrator they use. How does the choice of narrator influence your response to the character and events in each case?

IMPROVING SENTENCES:
Punctuating speech

To use dialogue, you need to be confident with different ways of presenting and punctuating speech. You may well be confident in putting 'he said' or something similar after the speech, but are you sure about putting it first, in the middle or even not using it at all?

Here is an extract from *Harry Potter and the Goblet of Fire* which features several different ways of presenting speech. Harry and Ron are trying to pluck up courage to ask girls out on a date.

> 'Who're you going with, then?' said Ron.
> 'Angelina,' said Fred promptly, without a trace of embarrassment.
> 'What?' said Ron, taken aback. 'You've already asked her?'
> 'Good point,' said Fred. He turned his head and called across the common room, 'Oi! Angelina!'
> Angelina, who had been chatting to Alicia Spinnet near the fire, looked over at him.
> 'What?' she called back.
> 'Want to come to the ball with me?'
> Angelina gave Fred an appraising sort of look.
> 'All right, then,' she said, and she turned back to Alicia and carried on chatting, with a bit of a grin on her face.
> 'There you go,' said Fred to Harry and Ron, 'piece of cake.'

Activity

Using the passage as an example, write out the rules of speech punctuation for:

- Putting 'he said' (or similar) last.

- Putting 'he said' (or similar) first.

- Putting 'he said' (or similar) in the middle.

It is assumed that the speech marks go around the actual spoken words.
You must define:
- What punctuation marks go between the spoken words and 'he said', and how you know which punctuation mark to choose.
- Where this punctuation goes.
- What happens if a sentence is broken in the middle by 'he said'.

- What happens if the speaker carries on to start a new sentence.

When you have completed this, see the answers on page 132, then try to punctuate these sentences:

Eventually we managed to charge it to Mrs Malone's account said Emily grinning. It's all right, she'll never notice.

One would have credited her with more tact, exclaimed Ned, furious, than to call on the first day of our honeymoon.

From *Not That Sort of Girl* by Mary Wesley

Task

There is nothing wrong with putting the speaker tag at the end, but if it is the only option you ever use, your writing will inevitably become repetitive and dull.

Try putting the speaker tag before the speech, or embedded within a speech.

Activity

Compose some examples in groups of three:

The first person starts a leading sentence on paper.

e.g. *"If the Martians land tomorrow,"*

The second person inserts who said it and how,

e.g. *said the Headmaster gravely,*

The third person completes the speech,

e.g. *"there will be an extended assembly."*

Swap positions for three turns.

Research

Activity

Open a novel and find a few pages of dialogue. Study where, when and why the writer is able to leave out any reference to who is speaking, and assume that the reader can work it out for themselves.

NARRATIVE STYLE:
Building tension

Writers build tension to engage the reader's deepest feelings of anticipation and fear.

 Activity

In this scene, Winston – the hero – is being tortured by threatening him with the thing he fears most: rats. The writing is carefully structured to build up the tension. The paragraphs are out of order. Put them in the right order by tracing the growing tension erupting into panic.

A – The circle of the mask was large enough now to shut out the vision of anything else. The wire door was a couple of hand-spans from his face. The rats knew what was coming now. One of them was leaping up and down, the other, an old scaly grandfather of the sewers, stood up, with his pink hands against the bars, and fiercely snuffed the air. Winston could see the whiskers and the yellow teeth. Again the black panic took hold of him. He was blind, helpless, mindless.

B – There was an outburst of squeals from the cage. It seemed to reach Winston from far away. The rats were fighting; they were trying to get at each other through the partition. He heard also a deep groan of despair. That, too, seemed to come from outside himself.

C – O'Brien picked up the cage and brought it across to the nearer table. He set it down carefully on the baize cloth. Winston could hear the blood singing in his ears. He had the feeling of sitting in utter loneliness. He was in the middle of a great empty plain, a flat desert drenched with sunlight, across which all sounds came to him out of immense distances. Yet the cage with the rats was not two metres away from him. They were enormous rats. They were at the age when a rat's muzzle grows blunt and fierce and his fur brown instead of grey.

D – The mask was closing on his face. The wire brushed his cheek. And then – no, it was not relief, only hope, a tiny fragment of hope. Too late, perhaps too late. But he had suddenly understood that in the whole world there was just one person to whom he could transfer his punishment – one body that he could thrust between himself and the rats. And he was shouting frantically, over and over.

E – 'I have pressed the first lever,' said O'Brien. 'You understand the construction of this cage. The mask will fit over your head, leaving no exit. When I press this other lever, the door of the cage will slide up. These starving brutes will shoot out of it like bullets. Have you ever seen a rat leap through the air? They will leap onto your face and bore straight into it. Sometimes they attack the eyes first. Sometimes they burrow through the cheeks and devour the tongue.'

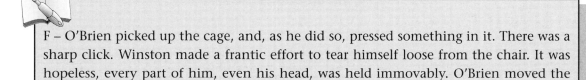

F – O'Brien picked up the cage, and, as he did so, pressed something in it. There was a sharp click. Winston made a frantic effort to tear himself loose from the chair. It was hopeless, every part of him, even his head, was held immovably. O'Brien moved the cage nearer. It was less than a metre from Winston's face.

G – 'Do it to Julia! Do it to Julia! Not me! Julia! I don't care what you do to her. Tear her face off, strip her to the bones. Not me! Julia! Not me!'

H – 'It was a common punishment in Imperial China,' said O'Brien as didactically as ever.

I – The cage was nearer; it was closing in. Winston heard a succession of shrill cries which appeared to be occurring in the air above his head. But he fought furiously against his panic. To think, to think, even with a split second left – to think was the only hope. Suddenly the foul musty odour of the brutes struck his nostrils. There was a violent convulsion of nausea inside him, and he almost lost consciousness. Everything had gone black. For an instant he was insane, a screaming animal. Yet he came out of the blackness clutching an idea. There was one and only one way to save himself. He must interpose another human being, the body of another human being, between himself and the rats.

J – 'The rat,' said O'Brien, still addressing his invisible audience, 'although a rodent, is carnivorous. You are aware of that. You will have heard of the things that happen in the poor quarters of this town. In some streets a woman dare not leave her baby alone in the house, even for five minutes. The rats are certain to attack it. Within quite a small time they will strip it to the bones. They also attack sick or dying people. They show astonishing intelligence in knowing when a human being is helpless.'

From *1984* by George Orwell

Find the correct order on page 132.

Discuss what features of the style helped you to place the paragraphs in order of growing tension.

Discuss the following points:

- O'Brien's speeches are quite measured and factual, so how do they contribute to the tension-building?

- Look particularly at the change in the length and pace of the sentences.

- Notice how the story moves between events, thoughts and speech.

- What equivalent methods are used to build up tension in film and television? Think of the scariest moments of *The X Files* or horror programmes.

Add two new paragraphs in to the passage, adjusted to the level of tension at that point.

Insert one paragraph after paragraph F, beginning: The cage was so close that Winston could smell …

Add another paragraph after paragraph H, beginning: Winston could bear no more.

THE ART OF ANALYSIS:
Analysing vocabulary choices

It is easy to go through a passage picking out examples of unusual and powerful vocabulary. To go a step further, you can begin to generalise about the choices made. Here, for example is a passage from which several verbs have been deleted. Discuss what they might be and make your own suggestions:

> We went to the shop and bought sherbet and sucked it through sticks of liquorice. _____ gently, the sherbet merely _____ the tongue; too hard, and you _____ with sweet powders; or if you blew back through the tube the sherbet-bag burst and you _____ in a blizzard of sugar. Sucking and _____, coughing and _____, we _____ our way down the lane. We drank at the spring to clean our mouths, then _____ water at each other and made rainbows. Mr Jones's pond was _____ with life, and covered with great white lilies – they _____ from their leaves like candle-fat, ran molten, then _____ on the water. Moorhens plopped, and dabchicks _____, insects rowed and _____. New-hatched frogs hopped about like flies, lizards _____ in the grass. The lane itself was _____ with cow-dung, hard baked and smelling good.

From *Cider with Rosie* by Laurie Lee

Once you have completed the task, read the original on page 132. The verbs used by the writer are very powerful – but how?

Activity

Find examples of verbs used in the passage that are particularly apt because:

- They sound like the thing described (onomatopoeic).

- They are expressed in terms of something else (e.g. animals behaving like humans).

- They are exaggerated to be larger than life.

- The verbs alliterate with nearby words in the sentence (start with the same sound).

To analyse a passage, look for patterns in the choice of:

- Verbs or any other word class, e.g. adjectives, adverbs.

- Bias, positive or negative attitude.

- Words that appeal to the senses, e.g. colours.

- Simile, metaphor and personification.

- Sounds, e.g. rhyme, alliteration, onomatopoeia.

- The degree of formality, e.g. colloquial, jargon, formal standard English.

Now read the writer's description of winter. Analyse the choice of vocabulary, and identify two or three patterns.

> The frost moon rose through the charcoal trees and we knew that we'd played too long. It was night now, and we were frightened. The beech wood was a cavern of moonlight and shadows, and we kept very close together. The dead sticks on the ground were easily seen, glittering with the night's new frost. As we ripped them from the earth, scabbed with soil and leaves, our hands began to burn with the cold. The wood was silent and freezing hard, white and smelling of wolves. Such a night as lost hunters must have stared upon when first they wandered north into the Ice Age.

From *Cider with Rosie* by Laurie Lee

Try writing a paragraph about autumn or spring in the same style.

MANAGING INFORMATION:
Telling, reporting and showing

Remind yourself of events so far in previous units. Carol now heads for the spot where the boy was found. But she is not alone, a BBC reporter, Angus Gold, and his camera crew are also there.

1) A Bulgarian hunter:
   Q. When did you first see the boy?
   A. I saw a group of wolves by a stream. The boy was about ten yards downstream and he was drinking at the same time.
   Q. So was he with the wolves in your opinion?
   A. He was close and they weren't attacking him.
   Q. So you assumed the wolves had looked after him.
   A. They were together. And after all, how else could he have survived so long if he had not been looked after? What more can I say?

2) A Professor of zoology, Professor Ernst:
   Q. Is it true that brown wolves will adopt abandoned children?
   A. There are two known cases. In both cases the mother wolf had lost cubs in some way. The children had taken their place.

   Q. Does this seem to you to have happened in this case?
   A. It is hard to say. The child was near wolves but could not be linked with one wolf in particular.
   Q. In the known cases, how long were the children with wolves?
   A. In one case eight years, another twelve.

3) The British consul, Mark Pearson:
   Q. Do you believe the boy is David Brewster?
   A. He might be. He is the right age.
   Q. In appearance is he similar?
   A. Very hard to say. The last picture of him was taken over ten years ago.
   Q. Are there no distinguishing characteristics?
   A. His passport said he had a small scar above his eyebrow. And before you ask, yes there is a slight scar above his eyebrow but there are many other scars as well.
   Q. From living in the wild?
   A. Quite possibly.

Angus has to give a 60 second story to camera for the nine o'clock news. As a reporter, he must distinguish between opinion and proven fact. Sometimes, he can't be sure of the truth, and on these occasions he must say so.

There is some information he can *tell* the viewer:

- Factual information.

There are other things he can *show directly*:

- Pictures of the place, photographs.

- Interviews.

There is some information he can *report*.

- Second hand information, but he must start with 'Some people say …' or 'Experts report …' or a similar expression.

Angus plans his script:

1 Open with question to engage viewer, e.g. 'Is the child found with wolves the missing …?'

2 Fill in background to the case.

3 Update on latest developments.

4 Theories about the boy.

5 What happens next.

6 Closing comment, 'This is Angus Gold for the nine o'clock news in Carpathia …'

Activity

- Discuss whether each item should be told, shown or reported.

- Consider whether Angus has the right material and information to do it this way.

- Write the script or prepare prompt notes and record it directly onto video.

To be continued in the next unit …

SPELLING:
Polysyllabic words

Long words are easier to spell if you break them up into their separate syllables, e.g. re/mem/ber.

Activity

- Divide the following words into syllables. The first two have been done for you:

diff/er/ence	sep/a/rate
business	temperature
marriage	reference
interest	necessary
peculiar	opportunity
immediately	unfortunately
extravagantly	extremely
advertisement	qualification

- Write them out in lists according to the number of syllables they contain e.g. two syllable words, three syllable words, etc.

- Now try to define what a syllable is.

- Can you think of ways which would help you to learn how to spell these words? Group words together if you can find a common rule that will help you.

HINT

Notice how often longer words:

- contain shorter words or parts of words within them, e.g. 'differ' in **differ**ence; 'inter' in **inter**est

- are the result of extending shorter words, e.g. the word 'marry' becomes marr**i**age and the y changes to I.

- contain prefixes, suffixes and base words, e.g. UN+NATURAL+LY.

Activity

What *whole* words can you find in the words below (their letters must already be together and in the right order)?

BUSINESS
SEPARATE
IMMEDIATELY
UNFORTUNATELY

VOCABULARY:
Words as signposts

Ideas are linked together in sentences using connecting words or phrases. These act as signposts to the reader, explaining how one idea leads to the next.

Some indicate *cause and effect,*

e.g. The class fell silent **because** the teacher opened the door.

Some indicate *sequence,*

e.g. **First** lock the door **then** remove the key.

Some *qualify (limit or specify) meaning,*

e.g. I want everyone to stand up **except for** Sally.

In future, you can prepare for writing essays by making a list of useful words that will help you to vary your links between ideas.

For further information on connectives, see Unit Eight.

Activity

List more connecting phrases that are used to:

- indicate cause and effect

- indicate sequence

- qualify meaning.

Can you think of other connecting phrases which:

- give particular emphasis, e.g. in particular

- add to an idea,
  e.g. as well as

- illustrate an idea,
  e.g. such as.

Which kind of connecting phrases would come in useful for these writing tasks:

- An argument against fox hunting?

- How to apply make-up?

- Great sea battles?

READING BETWEEN THE LINES:
Stock characters

Writers use stock characters because they are instantly recognisable. They are stereotypes.

Activity

Which characters can you think of from books, film or television which seem to fit instantly into any of the following categories:

- evil villain?

- hard nut?

- amiable rogue?

- victim?

- glamorous and unattainable figure?

- everybody's best friend?

Think of different stock female characters, e.g.

- glamour girl

- mother figure

- beach babe.

Because these characters are stereotypes, they are instantly recognisable and the reader knows immediately how to respond to them. In this passage, Charles Dickens introduces a villain, Wackford Squeers. Squeers is a creep.

Mr Squeers' appearance was not prepossessing. He had but one eye, and the popular prejudice runs in the favour of two. The eye he had was unquestionably useful, but decidedly not ornamental: being of a greenish grey, and in shape resembling the fan-light of a street door. The blank side of his face was much wrinkled and puckered up, which gave him a very sinister appearance, especially when he smiled, at which times his expression bordered closely on the villainous. His hair was very flat and shiny, save at the ends, where it was brushed stiffly up from a low protruding forehead, which assorted well with his harsh voice and coarse manner. He was about two or three and

> fifty, and a trifle below the middle size; he wore a white neckerchief with long ends, and a suit of scholastic black; but his coat sleeves being a great deal too long, and his trousers a great deal too short, he appeared ill at ease in his clothes, and as if he were in a perpetual state of astonishment at finding himself so respectable.

● Find five words or phrases that warn us (some more directly than others) that he is a villain, e.g. 'villainous'.

● Find five details of his appearance that are designed to make him unappealing.

If Mr Squeers is a villain, then Smike is definitely portrayed as a victim.

Read the following description of him and list all of the ways in which Dickens suggests this. An example has been done for you.

longs for affection

> The boy glanced, with an anxious and timid expression at the papers, as if with a sickly hope that one among them might relate to him. The look was a very painful one, and went to Nicholas' heart at once; for it told a long and very sad history.
>
> It induced him to consider the boy more attentively, and he was surprised to observe the extraordinary mixture of garments which formed his dress. Although he could not have been less than eighteen or nineteen years old, and was tall for that age, he wore a skeleton suit, such as is usually put upon very little boys, and which, though most absurdly short in the arms and legs, was quite wide enough for his attenuated frame. In order that the lower part of his legs might be in perfect keeping with this singular dress, he had a very large pair of boots, originally made for tops, which might have been once worn by some stout farmer, but were now too patched and tattered for a beggar. Heaven knows how long he had been there, but he still wore the same linen which he had first taken down; for, round his neck, was a tattered child's frill, only half concealed by a coarse, man's neckerchief. He was lame; and as he feigned to be busy in arranging the table, glanced at the letters with a look so keen, and yet so dispirited and hopeless, that Nicholas could hardly bear to watch him.

There are many kinds of victim in literature: innocent children, underdogs. Can you think of more stock victims?

Which type is Smike?

IMPROVING SENTENCES:
Leaving the best till last

Explanation

A good writer thinks about the order in which information is revealed in sentences. You can keep the reader waiting for the key word or punchline. Here is a sentence which deliberately leaves the best till last:

> In mid-August, just before Harriet and Sam went to Edinburgh, Joe passed his driving test, first time. He came home, face flushed, trying to contain his euphoria, and failing.

In the first sentence, the 'first time' is put at the end, as one would in speech, as a proud boast, as though it's better than could have been expected. In the second sentence, most space is given over to his efforts to contain his feelings, and the short ending 'and failing' reflects how quickly and easily all his efforts came to nothing.

Now explain why the writer has delayed some information to the end of these sentences:

> The moment Emily reached the top diving board she knew she would never face the dizzying drop and would, after a few forward creeps, retreat to the steps – and go down.

> 'I wouldn't play around with guns, Madame Blavatski,' Seth said lightly. 'You just might end up dead.'

> For a moment in the semi-darkness of the castle vault, with a cry so faint that Vosper could only just catch the sound, a child was calling.

Sometimes a sentence is shaped to build suspense, so that the main point arrives with an added force.

Try it

Activity

Now try writing your own sentences using this technique.
Here are some endings you might use:

… the voice of doom.

… a trickle of blood.

… last chance.

… disgust.

… moment of my life.

… the lonely cry of the wolf.

Then experiment with this
paragraph, rearranging sentences
to draw in the reader, and lead
them to the conclusion.

MATT GROENING

Many people feel it is a waste of time watching television. This is proved wrong by one man. After a childhood in front of the television he had a dream but no job. He moved into a flat in Los Angeles and set himself on the road to fame and fortune with some cartoons. He was driven almost to despair by the conditions in which he was forced to live. But this was Matt Groening, and *The Simpsons,* the wittiest cartoon of modern times, was the result of his early efforts.

Research

Activity

Open a novel and pick a page. Find five sentences that end
strongly.

Go back to your last substantial piece of writing, and find one or
two sentences that could be rearranged to give more force to
their endings.

NARRATIVE STYLE:
Picking up the pace

Explanation

Writers often need to communicate pace, and so increase the speed of a passage. For example:

- To suggest the sound of a quickening pulse when someone is alarmed, frightened or tense.

- To reflect speed described in the passage, e.g. a race.

- To communicate stress, panic or urgency.

Writers use a number of techniques to speed up prose:

- Writing in short, breathless sentences.

- Creating a breathless effect by breaking up sentences with a lot of punctuation.

- Using exclamation marks to communicate urgency.

- Using short abrupt words.

- Using strong words which remind the reader of the speed and stress of the situation.

- Using repetition, as though something is being urged.

- Using alliteration, especially 'S' which suggests swift movement.

 Activity

Find at least two examples of each of these techniques being used in the passage opposite. This passage describes a boy who plucks up courage to make a dangerous dive through a dark underwater tunnel.

Afterwards complete the passage in two paragraphs: one in which he struggles to reach the air and the other in which he just makes it. Use the techniques described to create a fast, urgent pace.

He was in a small rock-bound hole filled with yellowish-grey water. The water was pushing him up against the roof. The roof was sharp and pained his back. He pulled himself along with his hands – fast, fast – used his legs as levers. His head knocked against something; a sharp pain dizzied him. Fifty, fifty-one, fifty-two... He was without light, and the water seemed to press upon him with the weight of rock. Seventy-one, seventy-two... There was no strain on his lungs. He felt like an inflated balloon, his lungs were so light and easy, but his head was pulsing.

He was being continually pressed against the sharp roof, which felt slimy as well as sharp. Again he thought of octopuses, and wondered if the tunnel might be filled with weed that could tangle him. He gave himself a panicky convulsive kick forward, ducked his head, and swam. His feet and hands moved freely, as if in open water. The hole must have widened out. He thought he must be swimming fast, and he was frightened of banging his head if the tunnel narrowed.

A hundred, a hundred and one... The water paled. Victory filled him. His lungs were beginning to hurt. A few more strokes and he would be out. He was counting wildly; he said a hundred and fifteen, and then, a long time later, a hundred and fifteen again. The water was a clear jewel-green all around him. Then he saw, above his head, a crack running up through the rock.

You can read the original in the story *Through the Tunnel* by Doris Lessing.

THE ART OF ANALYSIS:
Getting at implied meaning

Most literature has messages for the reader, but they are rarely stated baldly. This deceptively simple poem by Simon Armitage is heavily loaded with possible meanings:

Poem

And if it snowed and snow covered the drive
he took a spade and tossed it to one side.
And always tucked his daughter up at night.
And slippered her the one time that she lied.

And every week he tipped up half his wage.
And what he didn't spend each week he saved.
And praised his wife for every meal she made.
And once, for laughing, punched her in the face.

And for his mum he hired a private nurse.
And every Sunday taxied her to church.
And he blubbed when she went from bad to worse.
And twice he lifted ten quid from her purse.

Here's how they rated him when they looked back:
sometimes he did this, sometimes he did that.

Now work through it in detail:

And if it snowed and snow covered the drive
he took a spade and tossed it to one side.

- The poem begins with a conjunction – a joining word – 'and'. What is the effect of this?

- Who is 'he' and why are we never given his name?

- What impression is given by the verb 'tossed'?

And always tucked his daughter up at night.

- How does the verb 'tucked' contrast with the verb 'tossed' in the previous line?

And slippered her the one time that she lied.

- Why does this line surprise the reader?

> And every week he tipped up half his wage.
> And what he didn't spend each week he saved.
> And praised his wife for every meal she made.

- What is suggested here about the man's attitude towards money?

- Look at the expression 'tipped up'. What does this mean? What is the effect of the colloquial language? Where else in the poem have you already come across colloquial language?

- What is implied here about the role of the husband and wife in their house?

> And once, for laughing, punched her in the face.

- How does this line compare with the last line of the first verse?

- How does the poet try to make it shocking?

> And for his mum he hired a private nurse.
> And every Sunday taxied her to church.
> And he blubbed when she went from bad to worse.

- What is implied about the way the man treated his mother?

- What is implied by the verbs 'taxied' and 'blubbed'?

> And twice he lifted ten quid from her purse.

- What is the effect of the verb 'lifted'?

- How does this line undermine the three lines which precede it?

> Here's how they rated him when they looked back:
> sometimes he did this, sometimes he did that.

- The last line is understated – it does not express a judgement or give way to emotion. How does this leave the reader feeling?

At the end

- Find examples of repetition in the poem. What impression does it give of the way the poem is spoken or delivered?

- Discuss your reaction to the title.

Finally:

1 First, argue that the poet is urging us to treat the man sympathetically. Find evidence in the poem that this is so.

2 Next, argue that the poet is urging us to treat the man as despicable. Again, find evidence to support this.

3 Finally, argue that the poet has deliberately left us on a knife edge, remaining non-commital, and why he might have done this.

4 Which version seems most likely to you?

**MANAGING INFORMATION:
Create your own writing frame**

Remind yourself of events so far in previous units.

Carol's paper, *The Planet*, sponsors a doctor, Doctor Latimer, to travel to Christiansted to try to establish whether or not the boy did live with wolves. The doctor conducts a thorough physical investigation. But his results are puzzling: it is difficult to tell whether they indicate that the boy *did* live with wolves, or simply that he lived in the wild on his own.

	Doctor R. S. Latimer **Christiansted**
RESULTS	
Eyesight	
Seems to avoid all bright light. Seems 20% better adapted to night vision than the average human.	
Hearing	
Acute for low sounds such as paper rustling, but ignores loud music and traffic noise.	
Smell	
Very acute for raw meat as well as forest grasses. Is disgusted by the smell of anything artificial.	
Speech	
Cannot speak. Of the 26 letters, is most attracted to the letter 'P'. Makes low growling noise if afraid.	
Taste	
Will only drink fresh water, which he smells first. Likes all meats, even if cooked. While eating, will occasionally look up and about.	
Movement	
Prefers to be on all fours. Can stand straight, but only with difficulty.	
Overall health	
In reasonable health. Has scarring to his right leg and arm, about 10 years old. Has a more recent bite mark to his left calf. Hair contains a variety of insects such as fleas and nits.	
Attitudes	
Is frightened by prolonged eye contact of any kind. Recoils from human touch. Will not wear clothes except the loosest kind.	

Consider the evidence so far.

What clues point towards the boy being David Brewster?

What suggests he is not?

The British Consul in Christiansted, Mark Pearson, is interested in the doctor's report. If the wild boy is indeed David Brewster, then he could be returned to Britain, and his remaining family. Mark has been asked by the Foreign Office to report on the boy's state of well-being and the likelihood that he is indeed David Brewster. Carol offers him the doctor's report and the Consul incorporates this into a report for the Foreign Office.

Activity

Write the report which must be four paragraphs long and contain no more than 150 words.

1 Decide the topics of the four paragraphs.

2 Write a starter sentence for each paragraph.

3 Check that the starter links back to the last paragraph and forward to later ones.

4 Make sure the last paragraph gives clear answers to the two requests.

Story to be continued in the next unit …

SPELLING:
'ER', 'OR', 'IR', 'AR', 'UR' and 'RE' endings

Words ending in the 'R' sound are tricky because there are at least six common ways of representing that sound,

e.g. partner, actor, stir, peculiar, fur, metre.

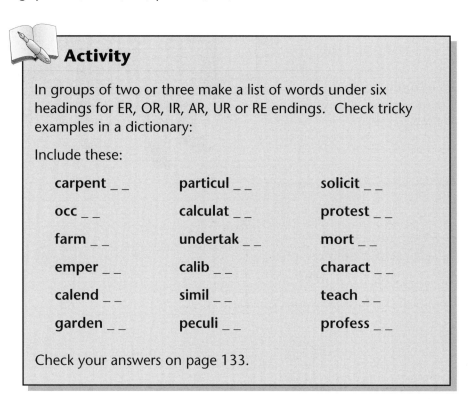

Activity

In groups of two or three make a list of words under six headings for ER, OR, IR, AR, UR or RE endings. Check tricky examples in a dictionary:

Include these:

carpent _ _	particul _ _	solicit _ _
occ _ _	calculat _ _	protest _ _
farm _ _	undertak _ _	mort _ _
emper _ _	calib _ _	charact _ _
calend _ _	simil _ _	teach _ _
garden _ _	peculi _ _	profess _ _

Check your answers on page 133.

Can you see any patterns, or anything that makes words more likely to appear in one group rather than another?

- Which ending is the most common and therefore the most likely?

- In which group are you likely to find words for which there is a French equivalent?

- In which group are you most likely to find adjectives?

- In which group are you likely to find the old-fashioned occupations?

- In which group are you likely to find the modern occupations?

- In which cases might the sound of the word help you?

VOCABULARY:
Small shades of meaning

A **synonym** is a word that has the same meaning as another word. But no two words mean *exactly* the same. Sometimes the meaning is slightly different, or it is more formal, or more general. Sometimes a word has overtones which give it a particular impact.

Consider the difference between:

HOME

ABODE

RESIDENCE

DWELLING

'Abode' and 'dwelling' are old-fashioned, and 'residence' is more formal than the word 'home'.

Define the subtle differences between these words and when you might use them:

WAGES	**CROCKERY**	**DRINK**
SALARY	**TABLEWARE**	**GULP**
INCOME	**DISHES**	**SWIG**
EARNINGS	**CHINA**	**SWALLOW**

Activity

Here is a list of words meaning NOISE. Some of them just mean NOISE, but some are types of sound. Sort them into two lists.

hubbub	screech	creak
clamour	uproar	rustle
commotion	wail	clanking
whine	pandemonium	tumult
clatter	din	cacophony

READING BETWEEN THE LINES: Symbols

A symbol is something which represents something else. Writers use symbolism when they want to suggest a deeper meaning for something. You will be familiar with visual symbols such as these. What do they symbolise?

The poet William Blake often uses symbolism in his poetry. Read his poem *The Garden of Love*.

The Garden of Love

I went to the Garden of Love,
And saw what I never had seen:
A Chapel was built in the midst,
Where I used to play on the green.

And the gates of this Chapel were shut,
And "Thou shalt not" writ over the door;
So I turn'd to the Garden of Love
That so many sweet flowers bore;

And I saw it was filled with graves,
And tombstones where flowers should be;
And priests in black gowns were walking their rounds,
And binding with briars my joys and desires.

Blake was a very religious man but religion was a very private matter for him. In this poem, he is critical of organised religion, which he sees as repressing human emotions.

 ### Activity

Think about what actually happens in this poem: the poet goes to a garden where he used to play as a child but everything has changed. Instead of flowers, there are briars, and the gates of the chapel are shut. What is it that Blake wants you to understand from the poem? Discuss this and work out what the following symbols might mean:

- The Chapel?

- The flowers?

- The briars?

- The graves and tombstones?

- The priests?

- The Garden?

What might Blake really be saying about organised religion in this poem?

Now read another poem by Blake. It is called *A Poison Tree*.

A Poison Tree

I was angry with my friend:
I told my wrath, my wrath did end.
I was angry with my foe:
I told it not, my wrath did grow.

And I water'd it in fears,
Night and morning with my tears;
And I sunned it with smiles,
And with soft deceitful wiles.

And it grew both day and night,
Til it bore an apple bright;
And my foe beheld it shine,
And he knew that it was mine,

And into my garden stole
When the night had veil'd the pole:
In the morning glad I see
My foe outstretch'd beneath the tree.

Activity

Write down what happens on a literal level in this poem. Then consider what, if anything, might be symbolic in the poem. The tree? The apple? What messages has Blake embedded in this poem?

IMPROVING SENTENCES:
Making verbs work harder

You already know about choosing among similar words to find the one that works best in your sentence. For example, choosing between 'yelled', 'shouted', 'screamed', 'cried' and 'called'. Here are two further things you can do to strengthen your verbs.

Use metaphorical verbs

A **metaphor** describes one thing in terms of another.

To use a metaphorical verb, choose a word which is commonly used to describe something else.

For example:

> 'Put down the gun,' he growled.

- 'Growled' is a metaphorical verb because it is normally used for bears.

- What other animal metaphors would fit here? (Think of snakes and pigs, for example.)

> The giant towered above us.

'Towered' is a metaphorical verb because a tower is not a person.

Explain what is implied if we describe:

- Someone scuttling away.

- Someone fishing in a drawer.

- Someone who lashes back in a conversation.

- A ship that slices through the waves.

Activity

Find the metaphorical verbs in the passage opposite, taken from *Truth or Dare*, by Celia Rees.

Suddenly, without any kind of warning, their car swerved violently, veering into the outside lane. The cars there were doing 80, 90 miles per hour and were practically nose to tail. Josh's stomach lurched and he sat frozen, gripping his seat. Everything seemed to slow as traffic juggled and slewed, brakes squealing, horns blaring. Car lights flashed in furious warning; drivers mounted curses through Plexiglas, faces white with their own fear. Josh's mother wrenched the wheel, this way, that way, sending her small car pinballing back across the carriageway.

From *Truth or Dare* by Celia Rees

Check your answers on page 133.

 Activity

Write six lines of dialogue in which an argument is taking place. Use at least three metaphorical verbs.

Put the verb first

Another powerful technique is to start a sentence with a verb. Try this first with any verb ending in 'ING.' For example:

Cradling the baby in his arms, Denny said his goodbyes.

Fluttering high above them in the sycamore tree was the lost kite.

Biting his lip, John decided it was time to go.

Don't overuse this technique.

You can also start a sentence with verbs ending in 'ED'. For example:

Tired of waiting, Kasim wandered off to see what was happening next door.

Covered in mud and grass, the dog looked even worse than before.

Notice the comma which is used when you get to the main clause.

NARRATIVE STYLE:
Descriptive detail

Descriptive detail is used by writers to conjure up pictures in the reader's mind. A well-placed detail can suggest a fuller picture, and provide insights into the characters and events of the story.

In this passage, a soldier describes the rubbish lining the streets of a French town towards the end of the war:

> All along the sides of the road, too, there is every kind of rubbish. Rubbish is not what most of it used to be, apart from the mess of broken brick and girders. These are all things from people's houses. You see a chair sticking out, spring coils from sofas and they are all charred and rusted. There are bedsteads and mattresses and piles of blood-stained clothing, part of a smashed wash-basin, children's toys. And then there is all the litter of the armies, of course. Everything has been left in the most appalling mess.

From *Strange Meeting* by Susan Hill

What does the detail of the rubbish tell you, and what feelings does it evoke?

Activity

In the following extract, Adam is staying at a country house, and is sitting in the library:

> There were several magazines in the library – mostly cheap weeklies devoted to the cinema. There was a stuffed owl and a case of early British remains, bone pins and bits of pottery and a skull, which had been dug up in the park many years ago and catalogued by Nina's governess. There was a cabinet containing the relics of Nina's various collecting fevers – some butterflies and a beetle or two, some fossils and some birds' eggs and a few postage stamps. There were some bookcases of superbly unreadable books, a gun, a butterfly net, an alpenstock in the corner. There were catalogues of agricultural machines and acetylene plants, lawn mowers, 'sports requisites'. There was a fire screen worked with a coat of arms. The chimney-piece was hung with the embroidered saddle-cloths of Colonel Blount's regiment of Lancers. There was an engraving of all the members of the Royal Yacht Squadron, with a little plan in the corner, marked to show who was who. There were many other things of equal interest besides, but before Adam had noticed any more he was fast asleep.

From *Vile Bodies* by Evelyn Waugh

Use the details of the passage to picture the library. Add the details onto a sketch like the one above.

What do you discover about the owner of the house from the details?

Activity

Imagine a mantelpiece or shelf – perhaps it is one you have at home. Picture it in your mind first and then draw a sketch using the outline below. It should suggest something about the person who lives there and uses it.

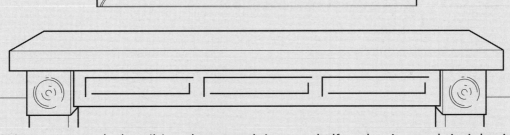

Write a paragraph describing the mantelpiece or shelf so that it reveals insights into the owner. Ask a partner to tell you what they can work out from the description and what impressions they get of the owner. Amend your writing to improve the impression.

Now try the same exercise with a top drawer in your own kitchen – the one where all the bits and pieces are kept!

THE ART OF ANALYSIS:
Focusing on the question

A good answer:

- clearly answers the question

- is succinct

- justifies its points.

A weak answer:

- doesn't answer this particular question

- wanders off the point

- asserts a point but doesn't explain or justify it.

In this passage, Ritie has just been reunited with her mother in Los Angeles after a long absence. The passage is followed by three questions.

I was as unprepared to meet my mother as a sinner is reluctant to meet his Maker. And all too soon she stood before me, smaller than memory would have her but more glorious than any recall. She wore a light-tan suede suit, shoes to match and a mannish hat with a feather in the band, and she patted my face with gloved hands. Except for the lipsticked mouth, white teeth and shining black eyes, she might have just emerged from a dip in a beige bath. My picture of Mother and Momma embracing on the train platform has been darkly retained through the coating of the then embarrassment and the now maturity. Mother was a blithe chick nuzzling around the large, solid dark hen. The sounds they made had a rich inner harmony. Momma's deep slow voice lay under my Mother's rapid peeps and chirps like stones under rushing water.

The younger woman kissed and laughed and rushed about collecting our coats and getting our luggage carted off. She easily took care of the details that would have demanded half of a country person's day. I was struck again by the wonder of her, and for the length of my trance, the greedy uneasinesses were held at bay. Years had to pass before I reflected on Momma's remarkable adjustment to that foreign life. She shopped in supermarkets larger than the town she came from. She dealt with accents that must have struck jarringly on her ears. She, who had never been more than fifty miles from her birthplace, learned to traverse the maze of Spanish-named streets in that enigma that is Los Angeles.

From *I Know Why the Caged Bird Sings* by Maya Angelou

1 What do we learn about Ritie's Mother in this passage? (5 marks)

2 How does the writer contrast her Mother and Momma in this passage? (3 marks)

3 How does the writer reveal her admiration and respect for Momma in this passage? (5 marks)

Weigh up the questions

1 Notice the balance of marks. They will help you to get the level of detail right. Tell yourself to offer a point for each mark.

2 Find the key words. In Question 1, it's easy to see 'Ritie's mother', but you also have to look for 'learn about'. It's a turn of phrase that includes not only what we are told, but what can be implied.

3 Study the instruction word. E.g. 'How' asks for an explanation.

Activity

Discuss what is meant by these question words:

DESCRIBE   EXPLAIN   COMPARE   CONTRAST

DISCUSS   CONSIDER   TRACE

One reason why many students lose marks is that they stray from the question. They start to answer a question which has not been asked or end up retelling the story.

Read the following two answers to Question 1.

Answer A

In this passage we learn about Mother's appearance and personality. She is a young woman, wearing a 'light-tan suit', matching shoes and a hat and gloves. She seems smart and fashionably dressed. She is an attractive woman with her 'lipsticked mouth, white teeth and shining black eyes' and Ritie seems quite dazzled by her, almost entranced. Mother seems delighted with the reunion since she 'kissed and laughed and rushed about' and her sense of energy and efficiency is revealed as we are told she 'easily took care of details that would have demanded half of a country person's day.'

Answer B

In this passage, Ritie is reunited with her Mother. They seem to have been apart for a long time and the reunion is very emotional. Ritie's Mother is contrasted to Momma who is described as a mother hen. Ritie seems embarrassed although when she looks back as an adult she understands how difficult it must have been for Momma. Ritie is pleased to be reunited with her Mother but I think she will miss Momma when she goes back to Arkansas.

- Discuss which answer is best and why. Also discuss where the other answer went wrong.

- Now write your own answers to Questions 2 and 3.

MANAGING INFORMATION:
Moving from information to commentary

Remind yourself of events so far in previous units.

Because of the intense public interest in the case of David Brewster, Carol is asked to write an extended article for the Sunday paper on the wider subject of feral children. She researches past cases on the internet.

The article will allow her to comment as well as report the facts.

Example

Information

- Keeps to facts.

- Avoids expressing opinions.

- Presents information and leaves the reader to work out what it all means.

> **INFORMATION: WILD PETER**
>
> In 1724, near the German town of Hamelin, a boy, described as a naked brownish black-haired creature, was seen running up and down in the fields. The boy was enticed into town, and once there immediately became a subject of great interest. He behaved like a trapped wild animal, eating birds and vegetables raw, and when threatened, he sat on his haunches or on all-fours looking for opportunities to escape. Peter was soon made the possession of King George of England, where he lived the rest of his life. During his life Peter never learned to talk, showed a complete indifference to money or sex, and was never seen laughing. However he loved music, could be taught a number of menial tasks, and when he once got lost, he found his own way back home. Peter died in 1785.

Commentary

- Interprets facts.

- Presents facts as part of an argument, a line of thought or point of view.

- Offers opinions (but is not necessarily opinionated).

- Follows or comes in addition to information.

> **COMMENTARY: WILD PETER**
>
> Like other wild children, Peter never took his full place in society, even after rescue. He could not shrug off the habits of diet and behaviour acquired in the wild. Although he loved music, he showed little interest in improving his social skills and so remained an oddity.

Activity

- Discuss in what ways the commentary is *commenting on* and *interpreting* the facts.
- Now take the information about one of the other wild children and write a short commentary on the case.

VICTOR, THE WILD CHILD OF AVEYRON

Victor, a boy of about 11 or 12, was discovered foraging for roots and acorns in the woods near Aveyron, France in 1799. Victor was taken to Paris, where he appeared to be human only in appearance. Victor behaved like an animal, ate rotten food with pleasure, was incapable of distinguishing hot from cold, and spent much of his time rocking back and forth like a caged animal. Victor was taken into the care of the brilliant scientist, Dr Jean-Marc-Gaspard Itard, who dedicated himself to the education of the boy. Victor proved to be a very difficult subject. Over the years, Victor only learned two terms, 'lait', (milk) and 'oh Dieu' (Oh, God). His sense of touch seemed to be far more important than his sense of sight, he did not demonstrate an ability to distinguish right from wrong, and like Peter before him, he was indifferent to sex. He did however, learn some menial tasks, such as setting a table. Victor lived the rest of his life in the care of his housekeeper, and died in 1828 at the age of 40.

THE INDIAN WOLF GIRLS

In a modern version of the Romulus and Remus story, two young girls were discovered under the care of a she-wolf in 1920, in Godamuri, India. The girls were taken to an orphanage in Midnapore (now part of Orissa). The children, Kamala, aged eight and Amala, aged 18 months, behaved exactly like small wild animals. They slept during the day and woke by night. They remained on all-fours, enjoyed raw meat, and were given to biting and attacking other children if provoked. They could smell raw meat from a distance, and they had an acute sense of sight and hearing. The youngest child, Amala, died one year later, but Kamala lived for nine years in the orphanage until she died of illness at the age of 17. Kamala did acquire a small vocabulary, but she remained very different to other children until the time of her death.

Story to be continued in the next unit …

SPELLING:
'ER', 'OR', 'AR', 'IR', 'UR' and 'RE' in the middle of words

When these letters come at the *end* of words they usually sound the same. This is not the case when they appear in the *middle* of words.

Activity

- Say these words out loud:

  squirm   **or**ganise   p**er**fect

  b**ar**gain   f**or**tunate   t**ur**bulence

  em**er**ge   agg**re**ssion   disc**ar**d

  m**ur**mur   m**ur**derous   conf**ir**m

- Which combinations still sound like 'ER' in 'germ'?

- Which can be distinguished by their own unique sound?

- Brainstorm further words to see if they keep to this pattern.

- Identify any words containing the 'ER' sound which give you trouble, and invent a way to remember the correct spelling (for example drawing a picture or inventing a sentence containing the same spelling combination).

Activity

Assonance is the word we use to describe the repetition of the same sound in the middle of words. It is like rhyme but in the middle of words,
e.g. Urgent murmurs confirmed that she was emerging from the church.

- Invent two sentences containing only the 'AR' and 'OR' sounds.

VOCABULARY:
Get and take

There are several phrases which use the verb 'get' followed by a preposition, e.g. get going, get by, get along.

Activity

- List as many phrases as you can that use 'get' plus a preposition.

- Now try to think of **synonyms** (words that mean the same or nearly the same) as these 'get' phrases: e.g. get going = start.

- Working in twos or threes, work out the 'get' phrase that goes with each of these verbs:

cope	bypass
descend	escape
mount	shirk
convey	blame
retrieve	agree
assemble	

- Make another list of phrases, this time using 'take' plus a preposition or even plus a noun, e.g. take cover.
- For each phrase, suggest a synonym.

READING BETWEEN THE LINES: The significance of endings

Narrative endings are important because they pass judgement on the characters and put the events in context. In a traditional ending:

- Good triumphs.

- Virtue is rewarded, for example with success, love or money.

- Evil is defeated.

- Villains are punished, for example with death or imprisonment.

- Victims are saved.

- Mysteries are solved.

- Wrongs are put right.

- Threats are removed.

- Loose ends are tied up.

In a traditional ending the world is put right. In life, and in some less traditional endings, this does not happen. Think of stories in which:

- the ending is left open, the threat not quite removed

- the villain gets away with it

- the hero doesn't get the heroine

And can you think of other untraditional endings?

Endings can be given extra impact if the writer:

- provides a surprise or twist ending

- withholds information until the very end

- provides the reader with some clues so that they can try to predict the ending

- reveals new information at the end of the story

- leaves the ending unresolved.

Activity

Read the following story by Kevin Crossley-Holland.

She didn't like it at all when her father had to go down to London and, for the first time, she had to sleep alone in the old house.

She went up to her bedroom early. She turned the key and she locked the door. She latched the windows and drew the curtains. Then she peered inside her wardrobe, and pulled open the bottom drawer of her clothes press; she got down on her knees and looked under the bed.

She undressed; she put on her nightdress.

She pulled back the heavy linen cover and climbed into bed. Not to try to read but to try to sleep – she wanted to sleep as soon as she could. She reached out and turned off the lamp.

There is only one more line to this story.

• Write down what the line might be if this is a traditional ending.

• Write down what the line might be if this is not a traditional ending.

Turn to page 133 for the writer's actual ending, then:

• discuss how expected or unexpected you found it

• identify five ways in which the writer braces the reader for a chilling conclusion

• list five ways in which the writer ensures that the ending still comes as a shock.

Look at page 133 for answers once you have tried for yourself.

IMPROVING SENTENCES:
Asides and extras

Asides

Occasionally, it can be effective to extend a sentence by dropping extra information into the middle. The effect is something like an 'aside' in drama.

For example:

The shark, <u>distracted by the sudden flurry above</u>, circled away from the boat and moved closer.

The underlined section is a clause: a short sentence, with its own noun and verb, which has been dropped into the middle of another sentence. It would be easy to think of the commas as brackets, because they sound like brackets. The rest of the sentence would make sense without the extra clause. It is known as an **embedded clause** because it is embedded in the main sentence.

Activity

Find the **three** embedded clauses in this passage about an attic:

> Josh fought his way round a ring of high-backed chairs, thin on the arms, that clustered round a coffee table topped with cracked glass and piled high with lethal electrical appliances, broken irons, and different kinds of fires.
>
> There were suitcases full of his clothes. Model boats, broken masted and rigged with cobwebs, leaned against boxes of other stuff: bits of old uniform, a military cap he must have worn in the war, all kinds of other military memorabilia, and books. Josh blew the dust off boring looking hardbacks, bound in drab dark blue and olive green, volumes of military history.
>
> From *Truth or Dare* by Celia Rees

Embedded clauses are useful for descriptive writing because they suggest detail. They are also quick and easy because they don't need a whole sentence to themselves. They also sound sophisticated.

Continue the description of the attic, using embedded clauses to build in more detail.

Extras

Sometimes, a writer will extend a sentence to include a full sequence of events, allowing us to see each stage of a process adding new actions to the main sentence. For example:

> Druse now brought the butt of his rifle against his cheek by cautiously pushing the barrel forward through the bushes, cocked the piece, and, glancing through the sights, covered a vital spot of the horseman's chest.

Here the writer is showing us the stages of preparing the rifle for shooting. The basic sentence ends at 'cheek', but it is extended four times, to suggest that the whole sequence is like one action.

Activity

Read on and find more examples of extended sentences, and why they have been used:

> At that instant the horseman turned his head and looked in the direction of his concealed foe-man – seemed to look into his very face, into his eyes, into his brave, compassionate heart.
>
> Carter Druse grew deathly pale; he shook in every limb, turned faint, and saw the group before him as black figures, rising, falling, moving unsteadily in arcs of circles in a fiery sky. His hand fell away from his weapon, his head slowly dropped until his face rested on the leaves in which he lay.

From *The Horseman in the Sky* by Ambrose Bierce

Try writing the next sentence, using the same technique, in which the horseman turns away and rides off.

NARRATIVE STYLE:
Preparing for the ending

Explanation

One of the commonest criticisms of stories written in tests is that they start well but run out of steam and end lamely. Clever writers know that readers are looking forward to seeing how a story ends, and guessing ahead. It is wise to play to this anticipation by dropping clues, like a treasure trail. Instead of thinking of continuing the start, try to think of it as working up to the conclusion.

Example

Below is a complete short story.

- Work out the meaning of the final line. Check your answer on page 134.

- Reread the story and find seven clues preparing you for the conclusion.

- Scan the story yet again for individual words and phrases that have an unsettling effect on the reader and make you feel something is not quite right, even dangerous, e.g. 'wasn't so safe'.

- Find some objects which could be interpreted as symbols of the woman's condition.

She was standing by the river looking at the stepping stones and remembering each one. There was the round unsteady stone, the pointed one, the flat one in the middle – the safe stone where you could stand and look round. The next wasn't so safe for when the river was full the water flowed over it and even when it showed dry it was slippery. But after that it was easy and soon she was standing on the other side.

The road was much wider than it used to be but the work had been done carelessly. The felled trees had not been cleared away and the bushes looked trampled. Yet it was the same road and she walked along feeling extraordinarily happy.

It was a fine day, a blue day. The only thing was that the sky had a glassy look that she didn't remember. That was the only word she could think of. Glassy. She turned the corner, saw that what had been the old pavé had been taken up, and there too the road was much wider, but it had the same unfinished look.

She came to the worn stone steps that led up to the house and her heart began to beat. The screw pine was gone, so was the mock summer house called the ajoupa, but the clove tree was still there and at the top of the steps the rough lawn stretched away, just as she remembered it. She stopped and looked towards the house that had been

---

added to and painted white. It was strange to see a car standing in front of it.

There were two children under the big mango tree, a boy and a little girl, and she waved to them and called 'Hello' but they didn't answer her or turn their heads…

The grass was yellow in the hot sunlight as she walked towards them. When she was quite close she called again, shyly: 'Hello.' Then, 'I used to live here once,' she said.

Still they didn't answer. When she said for the third time 'Hello' she was quite near them. Her arms went out instinctively with the longing to touch them.

It was the boy who turned. His grey eyes looked straight into hers. His expression didn't change. He said: 'Hasn't it gone cold all of a sudden. D'you notice? Let's go in.' 'Yes, let's,' said the girl.

Her arms fell to her sides as she watched them running across the grass to the house. That was the first time she knew.

From *I Used to Live Here Once* by Jean Rhys

Try it

Here is the plot of a story: A girl has a dream that her twin appears and leads her silently away from her home, over the fields, to a mountain. They play, but the twin never speaks. The girl imagines she is a long lost sister. They continue up the mountain.

Ending 1:
The twin leads her into dark canyons, and they lose themselves in the dark places of the mountains. Night descends. Everything goes black. The girl is found dead on the mountain. The twin was Death.

Ending 2:
The girl leads her to the peak and then everything dissolves and the girl awakes from a deep sleep. She discovers from her mother that she was born a twin but the other one died at birth.

Ending 3:
The twin leads the girl to the body of a mountaineer who has fallen and is close to death. She rescues him.

Activity

Write three contrasting paragraphs, to suit each ending, for that part of the story where they are ascending the mountain but the air is becoming more chill. Prepare the reader for the turn of events.

THE ART OF ANALYSIS:
Patterns in sentences

We are used to talking about patterns that run through a poem. For example, patterns of rhyme, rhythm or repetition. Sentences in prose also have patterns.

Within one sentence, you can find patterns of:

- repetition
- rhythm
- alliteration
- imagery
- contrast
- voice – the way the voice rises and falls.

Among several sentences, you can also find patterns of:

- structure
- content
- length.

Read Martin Luther King's famous speech about civil rights made to a crowd of 200,000 people in America in 1963.

I say to you today, my friends, that in spite of the difficulties and frustrations of the moment I still have a dream. I have a dream that one day this nation will rise up and live out the true meaning of its creed: 'We hold these truths to be self-evident: that all men are created equal.'

I have a dream that one day on the red hills of Georgia the sons of former slaves and the sons of former slave-owners will be able to sit down together at the table of brotherhood.

I have a dream that one day even the state of Mississippi will be transformed into an oasis of freedom and justice.

I have a dream that my four little children will one day live in a nation where they will not be judged by the colour of their skin, but by the content of their character.

This will be the day when all of God's children will be able to sing with new meaning "My country 'tis of thee let freedom ring."

And if America is to be a great nation, this must become true. So let freedom ring from the prodigious hilltops of New Hampshire. Let freedom ring from the mighty mountains of New York. But not only that. Let freedom ring from every hill and molehill of Mississippi.

When we let freedom ring from every town and every hamlet, from every state and every city, we will be able to speed up that day when all God's children, black men and white men, Jews and Gentiles, Protestant and Catholics, will be able to join hands and sing in the words of that old Negro spiritual, 'Free at last! Free at last! Thank God almighty, we are free at last.'

Find examples of:

- repetition

- the use of contrasts

- patterns in the way sentences open

- patterns in the use of 'I' and 'We'

- patterns in the length of sentences

- patterns in the way sentences end.

Discuss why these sentence patterns are useful in a speech.

Now study the following speech, on a similar subject, made by Nelson Mandela in 1990 and comment on the patterns you find, and their effect.

We have waited too long for our freedom! We can no longer wait. Now is the time to intensify the struggle on all fronts. To relax our efforts now would be a mistake which generations to come will not be able to forgive. The sight of freedom looming on the horizon should encourage us to redouble our efforts. It is only through disciplined mass action that our victory can be assured.

We call on our white compatriots to join us in the shaping of a new South Africa. The freedom movement is a political home for you, too. We call on the international community to continue the campaign...

Our march to freedom is irreversible. We must not allow fear to stand in our way.

MANAGING INFORMATION:
Creative thinking

Remind yourself of events so far in previous units.

Public interest in the wild child grows, but Carol's readers are asking questions to which there are no definite answers:

> *How did it feel to live among wolves?*

> *How did the wolves come to adopt a boy?*

Sometimes we have to accept that we can never know the full truth. However, we can make a guess based on evidence, experience and knowledge. We can imagine what it would be like if it were to happen to us, by playing through the events in our imagination. We can do this through drama, story-telling and deliberate day-dreaming. This 'playing out' of events can give us a feel for what might have happened and test out a theory to see if it works in practice.

Carol tries to imagine what it must have been like for the two-year-old David Brewster, all alone in the middle of Carpathia until the wolves discovered and adopted him into their pack. She checks out a book for new parents describing what children are like, so that she will understand the mind of the two-year-old boy.

Age	Speech	Social	Movement
One year	May be able to say the names of a few objects, but understands many more. May have own jargon or 'scribble' language.	Understands that if you leave him you will come back. Enjoys games such as stacking beakers, posting shapes and pat-a-cake.	Crawls on hands and knees or on hands and feet, or may be a bottom-shuffler. Can stand up clinging to furniture or even walk alone. Picks up tiny things with thumb and finger. Uses a pencil to do circular scribbles.
Two years	Can put several words together and chatters. Uses the pronouns 'I', 'me' and 'you'. Sometimes echoes what is said.	Plays alone even if with other children. Likes to say 'no' and do the opposite of what you want. Enjoys exploring from a safe base.	Can easily start and stop running, and jumps with both feet. Can kick, throw a ball and walk on tiptoe. Draws straight lines and likes playing with building bricks. Can unscrew a lid and use a spoon. Slowly learns to use buttons, undress and wash hands.
Three years	Becoming much more fluent now, talking in sentences and using prepositions, such as 'with', 'from' and 'into', and plurals. Learns rhymes or stories by heart.	Beginning to share toys. May have a make-believe friend. Enjoys helping adults and is beginning to be able to wait for things more calmly.	Runs around corners and climbs. Goes upstairs like an adult, but comes down one step at a time. Can pedal a bicycle, draw figures, use a paintbrush and blunt-ended scissors. Uses a knife and can dress self.

Carol then tries to imagine the moment when the wolves discovered David at the age of two. Why didn't they kill the boy? What happened to the rest of his family? She hopes by writing things down she may be able to solve the mystery of how David survived.

The overturned Range Rover lay below in the narrow gorge. A young boy, unaware of the fate of his family, lay on the grassy knoll gurgling contentedly to himself.

Dark shapes moved in the bushes.

The young boy decided he was hungry. 'Drink all gone. Me more milk' but unusually no comforting voice and outstretched hand came into view. A vague feeling of puzzlement briefly touched the young child's consciousness.

The dark shapes became clearer. A grey wolf pack emerged in the clearing. The sunlight caught the silver grey of their fur as they came into view . . .

Activity

Continue in one of three ways:
- By closing your eyes and playing through the events in your mind.
- By telling the story to a partner.
- By continuing the writing.

Afterwards, discuss:
- What new light this imagining casts on the likely events.
- Whether it confirms or casts doubt on the 'raised by wolves' story.
- What kind of insights you can achieve by living through the events.

Story to be continued in the next unit …

SPELLING:
Words ending with 'TION', 'SION', 'SSION', 'SIAN' and 'CIAN'

These word endings are pronounced 'SHUN'.

Activity

- In groups of two or three, provide the endings of the following words.

persua_____	educa_____	posse_____
magi_____	admi_____	deten_____
comprehen_____	satisfac_____	musi_____
politi_____	produc_____	explo_____
mathemati_____	qualifica_____	organisa_____
reputat_____	discu_____	excep_____
rejec_____	permi_____	relat_____
po_____	Rus_____	Prus_____
exten_____	physi_____	promo_____
consump_____	percu_____	emo_____
corro_____	ero_____	deten_____
infla_____	commi_____	fic_____

- Which ending is the most common?
- Which ending is unique to place names?
- Which ending is usually added to base words ending in 'D' or 'S'?
- Which ending is usually added to base words ending in 'T'?
- Which ending is usually added to base words ending in 'MIT'?
- Which ending is added to base words ending in 'IC'?
- Which ending is used when there is a 'ZH' sound?
- Can you find other patterns?
- Can you find other, more unusual ways of spelling the 'SHUN' ending?

Check your answers on page 134.

VOCABULARY:
Nationality

 Activity

- Brainstorm a list of countries and nationalities, and work out the general rules for changing the name of the country to the name of the nationality,

  e.g. for England, you change the ending from 'and' to 'ish'.

England	$\longrightarrow$	English
Poland	$\longrightarrow$	Polish
Portugal	$\longrightarrow$	Portuguese
Russia	$\longrightarrow$	Russian

- Research also the names which countries use for themselves in their own language and their names in English,
  e.g.

Spain	$\longrightarrow$	Espana
Italy	$\longrightarrow$	Italia
France	$\longrightarrow$	France

- Consider why these differences have occurred.

 Activity

Find out how to say the following (very useful) terms in as many different languages as possible:

Hello

Goodbye

Thank you

Okay!

Help!

Can you see any similar words or parts of words? Why are there similar words?

READING BETWEEN THE LINES:
Hidden persuaders

ADVERTISEMENT PROMOTION

Spread the news

Olivio spread is not only delicious, creamy and light-tasting – it also brings you the health benefits of a Mediterranean diet

Why is it that people in the Mediterranean seem to enjoy life so much? Lots of sunny weather, an outdoor lifestyle and a relaxed attitude to everything make all the difference. Crucially, a diet of plenty of fresh vegetables, fruit, fish and olive oil, with a glass or two of wine along the way, means that Mediterraneans on the whole live longer than we do.

Olivio spread is made with pure Mediterranean olive oil, and is a great way of incorporating the goodness and benefits of olive oil into your diet. Most importantly, Olivio spread is absolutely delicious – it tastes light and creamy, and it's ideal just spread on to freshly baked bread. Olivio is also extremely versatile and perfect for use in recipes.

It's difficult at times to find the time and motivation to try to live healthily, but it should never come as too much of an effort to eat fresh, wholesome and delicious food. Try Olivio spread as part of a balanced diet and take a leaf out of the Mediterranean book of a balanced way of life.

If you have any comments or questions on Olivio spread, call the Careline free on 0800 616030, Monday to Friday, 9am to 5pm. Calls may be recorded.

Join Club 18 130

OLIVIO
WITH PURE MEDITERRANEAN
Olive Oil

Reading Between the Lines

1. Catching your eye

Study the advertisement for Olivio on the opposite page. It appeared in the May edition of the Sainsbury's Magazine. As you read it for the first time, pay attention to the behaviour of your eyes and brain: where do you look first and where is your attention drawn?

Activity

Draw a sketch of an advertisement like the one opposite on a separate sheet, circling the items that your eyes are drawn to, linked by arrows to show how you move your eyes about the page.

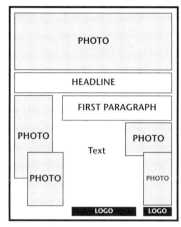

Buying butter is not your big interest in life. Promoters know this and work hard to gain your interest and attention. Your eyes are drawn in to the advertisement.

2. Images for your imagination

Study the pictures. The bread and the tub of Olivio are clearly reminding you of the product itself but what about the others? How are they linked to Olivio?

3. Key words for your memory

List key words that are repeated, underlining those that are repeated more than twice. These are repeated so that they stick in your memory.

4. Messages to your heart

Run your finger over the words of the advertisement and count up the number of 'positive' words it contains, e.g. 'delicious', 'health'.

The advertisement also speaks directly to the reader. Find three examples, and comment on the way this might increase the reader's interest in the product.

5. Arguments for your brain

The advertisement also puts forward some 'good sense' reasons for buying Olivio. Find them.

Activity

Find another advertisement and analyse how is makes its appeal using the five headings on this page.

IMPROVING SENTENCES:
Developing more sophisticated sentences

You know about joining ideas together in a sentence using a simple conjunction such as 'and', 'so', 'but' and 'because'. To build up more sophisticated sentences, there are three things you can do:

1. Use a range of interesting connectives

There are a number of connectives you can use to introduce and link ideas to suggest their sequence.

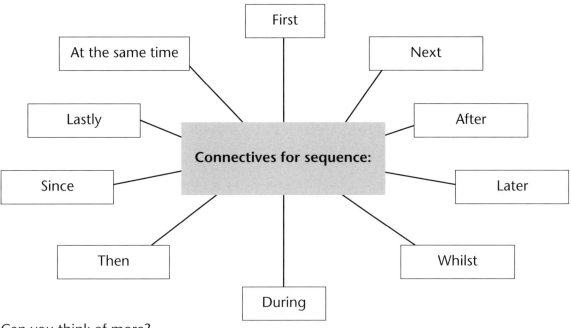

Can you think of more?

 Activity

Make list of at least five connectives you can use to link ideas in each of these ways:

- To introduce an example, e.g. for instance, as in the case of.
- To link cause and effect, e.g. because, as a result of.
- To qualify a point, e.g. except for, although.
- To emphasise a particular point, e.g. especially if, in particular.
- To add to or extend an idea, e.g. as well as, also.
- To compare ideas, e.g. in the same way, similarly.
- To contrast ideas, e.g. on the other hand, unlike.

Find helpful lists on page 135.
Don't rely on the same few connectives in your writing. Draw on your lists to use a variety.

2. Use subordinate clauses

Ideas which are joined by the word 'and' have equal weight. Other conjunctions can make one of the ideas dependent on the other.

Two equal sentences	Michael drove home in the car.
	David walked home.
One sentence but two equal ideas:	Michael drove home in the car *and* David walked.
One sentence containing one main idea and the other is dependent:	David walked home *because* Michael drove home in the car.

The conjunction 'because' makes the second idea dependent on the first for its meaning. You know it is dependent because it wouldn't make sense on its own: 'because Michael drove home in the car'. It is known as a **subordinate clause**.

The first section 'David walked home', by contrast, makes sense on its own. It is known as the **main clause**.

3. Vary the order of clauses

For a mature and sophisticated style, use a subordinate clause but move it from the back of the sentence to the front or drop it into the middle.

For example:

HELP

Clauses are mini-sentences with their own noun and verb. You can always spot a subordinate clause because there is a warning in the conjunction. A conjunction like 'because' warns you that the second clause can only make sense if it is read with the first.

Great writers use many subordinate clauses. Subordinate clauses allow you to write subtle and complex ideas, and to indicate *how* ideas are connected.

In spite of technical difficulties, Ferrari strived to win the race.

├ – – –subordinate clause first – – – – –┤

Ferrari strived, in spite of technical difficulties, to win the race.

├ – subordinate clause in middle – – –┤

Notice that when you move a subordinate clause forward in this way, commas are placed between it and the main clause.

Activity

Try writing a paragraph which describes a person arriving home alone at night to a power cut, entering the house and trying to find a way to light at least one room. Use some of the techniques explained in this section.

NARRATIVE STYLE:
Mind reading

Explanation

Writers have the power to take the reader inside the heads of their characters to hear their thoughts, sense what they are feeling and to see events from their perspective. The writer acts like God in these cases, because in real life, we can only guess what it is like to think and feel as someone else.

Taking the reader inside the mind of the character can:

- make the reader sympathise with the character

- help the reader to understand the character better

- make the character more real

- give inside information about motives and past events

- pause the action for a moment of peace and reflection

- slow the pace of the story

- heighten the drama and emotion of a key event

- show events as they are experienced rather than as a spectator.

Example

In this passage Andres is in a prison camp:

An old man appealed to the guards to permit him to go to the lavatory. He was ordered to use the bucket in the centre of the hut. He protested and they dragged him out. He did not return. From that moment no one argued against using the bucket. It overflowed but still the prisoners accepted: the stench and the crush were a small price to pay for holding on to the precious jewel of life.

Accept, accept – learn to accept. Where had Andres heard that? From Juan, no doubt. So Andres accepted. He laid his head on his knees. He seemed to have nodded off for hours, though real time had moved on scarcely seconds.

Andres lifted his cheek from his knee. He turned his face. He pressed his teeth into his knee: don't drift. Don't slip away. Fix Isa's smile over the goalposts of your brain. Goalposts! That's not bad, considering. Might make a song. How about that? She kissed me once on the goalposts of my brain. It's a winner.

Yet – pain, from a blow in the back by a rifle butt; cramp in the limbs, a throbbing head. Hold – hold on. Map the future. We'll tour... We'll write songs, skits, plays. We'll make people laugh and clap their hands. We'll sing songs of hope. We'll resist.

He could not hold the spirit in him long. He looked about him and the shout of his defiance was a whisper, feeble and uncertain. To think, somewhere out there the sun's rising as usual.

Soon after dawn, an officer arrived with a list. He read out a dozen names. 'You will accompany me.' He spoke to the guard who thrust his way between the squatting and crouching prisoners.

'Me?' Andres blinked up at the guard.

'On your feet!'

From *Talking in Whispers* by James Watson

Pick out:

- Those sentences which are straight forward narrative told by the narrator, showing events 'from the outside'.

- Those sentences which are words we can hear directly in Andres' mind.

- Those sentences in which the narrator tells us how Andres is feeling inside, but in the narrator's words rather than Andres' own words.

What does the reader gain from having this access into Andres' thoughts and feelings?

Try it

Activity

Imagine the officer takes Andres away, perhaps to be released, perhaps to be beaten or transferred.

- Write one paragraph to follow on immediately from the extract.

- Write another paragraph in which Andres learns what it is they are going to do with him.

In both paragraphs, use a mixture of the narrative perspectives listed above, as used in the extract.

THE ART OF ANALYSIS:
Finding your own words

Sometimes you know what something feels like, but it is hard to explain it in words. The task is to find the words that pinpoint the feeling or thought evoked and explain what the written text means.

Read the following poem by Seamus Heaney.

Blackberry Picking

Late August, given heavy rain and sun
For a full week, the blackberries would ripen.
At first, just one, a glossy purple clot
Among others, red, green, hard as a knot.
You ate that first one and its flesh was sweet
Like thickened wine: summer's blood was in it
Leaving stains upon the tongue and lust for
Picking. Then red ones inked up and that hunger
Sent us out with milk-cans, pea-tins, jam-pots
Where briars scratched and wet grass bleached our boots.
Round hayfields, cornfields and potato-drills
We trekked and picked until the cans were full,
Until the tinkling bottom had been covered
With green ones, and on top big dark blobs burned
Like a plate of eyes. Our hands were peppered
With thorn pricks, our palms sticky as Bluebeard's.

We hoarded the fresh berries in the byre.
But when the bath was filled we found a fur,
A rat-grey fungus, glutting on our cache.
The juice was stinking too. Once off the bush
The fruit fermented, the sweet flesh would turn sour.
I always felt like crying. It wasn't fair
That all the lovely canfuls smelt of rot.
Each year I hoped they'd keep, knew they would not.

Suppose you want to describe the season of the poem.

You are told it is late August in the first line, but you want to describe the mood, feel, atmosphere or quality of it. You catch the feel of it from the poet's words: 'heavy', 'thickened', 'sticky', 'glutting', 'stinking', 'fermented'. You need to find a word.

Fish for words by:

● Imagining the scene and saying to yourself 'It's so....' and wait for a word.

- Starting a line for your writing: 'The poet describes the mood of late August. It is …'

- Finding synonyms for some of the key words used by the poet and see if one will do, e.g. heavy – humid, close, overbearing, oppressive.

Find a sentence starter:

- If in doubt, keep it simple: 'The season is…'

- Try to mention the writer at work: 'The poet presents the season as…'

- Try to link to the previous point: 'The weather is…'

Example:

We are told at the outset that it is late August. The summer is at its height, and the atmosphere is <u>oppressive</u>. Everything is <u>over-ripe</u>: 'sticky', 'rotting' and 'heavy'.

Fill in suitable words here:

The colour red is mentioned repeatedly, and we are reminded of it in the words 'berry', 'wine', 'blood', and 'purple'. It evokes a sense of . . . . . .

The final stanza describes the rotting berries in the bath. The image of the berries covered in a 'rat-grey fungus, glutting' and stinking juices is deliberately . . . .

The ripeness of the first stanza is replaced with a sense of . . . .

 Activity

Now write a short paragraph – no more than three sentences in each one – tackling each of these two topics:

1 The way the writer has used body imagery in the first stanza
2 The setting or sense of place in the poem.

Have a go at writing your own poem, using some of the poetic features which Heaney employs in his poem. You might call your poem:

- Strawberry Picking

- Cutting Grass

- Beach Combing

MANAGING INFORMATION:
From bias to balance

Remind yourself of events so far in previous units.

PRESS RELEASE

Digital Pictures UK is proud to announce an *exciting new* film project this autumn. The remarkable true story of the boy who ran with wolves will be shot on location in central Europe and tells how a pack of grey wolves adopted the lonely two-year-old child on a bleak Carpathian roadside and the long years of harsh survival in the wild that followed. 'Wolf Boy' is a compelling story that will stir the emotions.

Digital Pictures is proud to tell the story of David Brewster's miraculous rescue, his long journey back to civilization, and the touching story of his growing friendship with the journalist who flew half-way round the world to help him to a better life.

PRESS RELEASE
DIGITAL PICTURES UK

Digital Pictures UK believe the campaign mounted against the company by *The Planet* newspaper is **malicious, unfair and probably illegal**. The incitement to boycott other *Digital* movies is causing great damage to a reputable film company with high ethical standards that has been a great success story in the film industry over the last decade. Winners of coveted Oscars last year, the company's reputation has been harmed by vindictive and unfounded slurs in *The Planet's* sustained campaign against us.

'Wolf Boy' is a film that will vividly portray the life of a remarkable young man. *Digital Pictures* will be donating money to a trust fund set up for David, but as we have repeatedly pointed out to *The Planet*, success in the film industry can never be guaranteed. The size of the fund will be dependent on the commercial success of the film. We urge the public to support our Wild Child fund by coming to see the film.

PLANET EDITORIAL

What rights do we have over our own life stories? None, it would seem, if the film industry has its way. We have all followed the heart-rending story of David Brewster, the wolf boy who was brought back to civilization: a story that was first told in these pages in a world exclusive report. Now *Digital Pictures UK* want to use the sketchy details of David's life for a movie.

But they have refused repeatedly to pay for the privilege.

Whatever happens to David in the future it will need money. Without a family, who we believe perished on a dangerous mountain road in Carpathia, he is a lonely boy who has little going for him.

Surely a successful Oscar-winning film company can do the right thing by the person whose life story they are exploiting?

Join the *The Planet's* FILM BOYCOTT and picket cinemas NOW!

Activity

Your task is to plan a balanced account of the argument between *Digital Pictures UK* and *The Planet*.

1 List the points put forward by each side.

2 Identify the main points.

3 Organise your account into seven paragraphs (two have been done for you).

Start by grouping points together. For example:

- A point linked with the response from the other side.
- Similar points bundled together.
- Extend one point with a closely-related point.

4 Devise the opening to each paragraph so that it indicates the topic of the paragraph and keeps the reader 'clued in' to who is saying what.

Paragraph topic	Paragraph opening
1 Introduction: the controversial film	Anger has flared over a plan to…
2 *The Planet's* main objections	*The Planet* newspaper has condemned the film because…

Afterwards, review:

- How you decide the order of points when there is no natural sequence.
- Useful connectives to use when you compare and contrast points of view.

For example:
- COMPARE: similarly, likewise.
- CONTRAST: on the other hand.

Story to be continued in the next unit …

SPELLING:
Borrowed digraphs

Some words contain unexpected and unusual groups of letters because they have been borrowed from other languages.

'RH'

The combination of the letters 'RH' in these words comes from the Greek:

rhythm, rhyme, diarrhoea, rhetoric

- Look up other words containing 'RH'

- One way of remembering how to spell these words is by using a **mnemonic** – a memory aid, e.g. rhythm helps your two hips move = rhythm. Compose mnemonics for two other 'RH' words.

'PN'

The French word for tyre is pneu.

Can you see a connection between a tyre and these two words?

pneumonia, pneumatic

'GUE' and 'QUE'

In both of these endings the 'UE' is not voiced.

GUE	QUE
fatigue	grotesque
intrigue	picturesque
colleague	statuesque
tongue	unique
meringue	mosque

- To help you learn these words, it might be useful to say the 'gew' or 'kew' sounds at the end of the words. It may sound funny, but it often works!

The language from which these endings were borrowed still uses these endings. Which language is it?

VOCABULARY:
Opposites

Antonyms or opposites can often be formed by adding a prefix:

e.g.

un	+	willing
ir	+	responsible
il	+	legal

Activity

- Find at least 10 prefixes which can be used to make an antonym and provide 3 examples of each.

- Identify any rules or patterns,
  e.g. IR is common to words beginning with R, e.g. reversible

More interesting antonyms can be created by finding alternatives words,

e.g.

| optimist | – | pessimist |
| elevate | – | depress |

Activity

Find antonyms for the following adjectives *without* using the prefix method.

- *Inspiring* book

- *Relaxed* attitude

- *Responsible* behaviour

- *Informal* discussion

- *Patronising* tone

READING BETWEEN THE LINES:
What's so funny?

Humour has always been popular in fiction, but factual writing has tended to be serious, because it is put forward as the truth, and not to be undermined. Most humour depends on putting something quite ordinary in the wrong or unexpected context. In this extract, the writer gets a laugh out of introducing unexpected comments and details into factual writing:

1964 Britain invades America ... with four young men called The Beatles! Their weapons? Pop music. (At least the Brits can do something right.) The Americans reply by sending the incredible Sindy Doll over here. She has British boy 'Action Man' to keep her company (or run her over in his Action Jeep). In South Africa the government locks up a man called Nelson Mandela and will keep him locked up for 25 years. His real crime is to fight for equal rights for the black people in his country.

1965 Shocking young women wear something called the 'mini-skirt'. Sir Winston Churchill dies (no connection). There is a 70 m.p.h. speed limit on roads and police Panda cars to catch the villains who dare to go faster. Home video-recorders are on sale and within 20 years some people will know how to use them properly.

1966 England's football team win the World Cup. They beat Germany in the final. This is a bit unfair because they have beaten Germany in two wars. It's about time they let the Germans win.

Activity

- Identify the elements that are out of place in the factual writing and therefore funny.

- Pinpoint exactly what is inappropriate about each item.

- What knowledge would you need to have already to make sense of the jokes? (E.g. knowing that most people have difficulty setting a video recorder.)

- Who is the intended reader and how do you know?

- How far is this kind of humour one big 'in-joke'?

Here are several more extracts from the same book.

GRUESOME FIND

Cornwall. Builders made a grisly find when they restored an attic in a Falmouth house on 20 December 1976. It was a human arm. They didn't report it but left it for the scaffolders. When the scaffolders arrived they failed to report it too and left it in the road. Finally a shocked passer-by called the police who said the mummified arm had belonged to a woman and could be anything from five to 100 years old. The arm still had a note attached – a little joke left by the builders. It said, 'In case you need a hand!' But who owned that arm, how did she die, and who killed her?

Singer Sam Cooke was a friend of heavyweight boxing champ, Muhammed Ali. He was also as fast on his feet until one night in 1964 he was hit by something faster. What?
a) A Greyhound bus when he jumped into the road to wave it down.
b) A bullet from the gun of a woman he'd upset.
c) A brick dropped from the roof of a skyscraper.

Answer
b) He died, by the way. One of his greatest hits was You Send Me. She did that all right.

From *Horrible Histories: The 20th Century*, Scholastic

Activity

- Analyse the source of humour in these two extracts.

- Discuss what is meant by 'sick' humour.

- Choose an important piece of factual information from the last five years and present it in the same humorous style.

IMPROVING SENTENCES: Rhetorical questions

Explanation

Rhetorical questions are those which do not need or expect a direct answer from the listener. They are used to grab the attention, a stylish way of presenting a statement in an active engaging way.

A rhetorical question is also a leading question. The answer is often obvious and inevitable, and the one preferred by the speaker. However, it has the effect of making the audience respond privately. It feels as if the speaker has appealed to one's common sense. Sometimes a rhetorical question is used in a speech so that the speaker can give the answer.

Examples

What is the expected but unspoken answer to these rhetorical questions?

'Have you ever stood in a freezing river at 5 o'clock in the morning by choice?'

'Is it not crystal clear, then, comrades, that all the evils of this life of ours spring from the tyranny of human beings?'

From *Animal Farm* by George Orwell

'But is this simply part of the order of nature? Is it because this land of ours is so poor that it cannot afford a decent life for those who dwell upon it? No, comrades, a thousand times no!'

From *Animal Farm* by George Orwell

Virgin Territory
We have Virgin Cola, Virgin Rail, Virgin Mobile (phones), Virgin Radio, Virgin Brides, Virgin Airlines, Virgin One (financial services) and now Richard Branson wants the Lottery.
　　Any plans afoot to rename Britain the Virgin Isles?

Letter to *Daily Mail* from Gill Wright, Bridgewater, Somerset.

Hath not a Jew eyes? Hath not a Jew hands, organs, dimensions, senses, affections, passions? Fed with the same food, hurt with the same weapons, subject to the same diseases, healed by the same means, warmed and cooled by the same winter and summer, as a Christian is? If you prick us, do we not bleed? If you tickle us, do we not laugh? If you poison us, do we not die? And if you wrong us, shall we not revenge? If we are like you in the rest, we will resemble you in that.

From *The Merchant of Venice* by William Shakespeare

That man over there says a woman needs to be helped into carriages and lifted over ditches and to have the best place everywhere. Nobody ever helped me into carriages or over mud puddles or gives me a best place, and ain't I a woman?

Transcript of speech by Sojourner Truth, 1852

Can't a critic give his opinion of an omelette without being asked to lay an egg?

Clayton Rawson, quoted by Frank Muir in *Frank Muir goes into Investigation*

Research

Writing that wants to persuade an audience might use rhetorical questions.

Find examples of rhetorical questions in those parts of newspapers where a point of view is expressed, e.g. editorials, letter pages, opinion articles.

Try it

 Activity

Take the following statements and convert them into rhetorical questions for a speech:

It is wrong to use animals for scientific research. Inflicting pain and needless suffering on defenceless creatures cannot be right. Man, supposedly the most advanced and sophisticated creatures on this planet, kills without conscience and defends his actions by arguing it is in the interests of scientific enquiry.

Rhetorical questions are few and far between in writing, but more common in speeches. Why do you think this is the case?

NARRATIVE STYLE:
Short sentences

Explanation

Writers sometimes revert to short, incomplete sentences. It mimics the way people behave when they are stunned, cracking up or too numb to speak. On these occasions, the reader has to work hard to piece together the sentences and work out what lies beneath them.

Example

In this extract, the doctor's son has watched his father helping at a difficult birth and a suicide.

> 'Do ladies always have such a hard time having babies?' Nick asked.
>
> 'No, that was very, very exceptional.'
>
> 'Why did he kill himself, Daddy?'
>
> 'I don't know, Nick. He couldn't stand things, I guess.'
>
> 'Do many men kill themselves, Daddy?'
>
> 'Not very many, Nick.'
>
> 'Do many women?'
>
> 'Hardly ever.'
>
> 'Don't they ever?'
>
> 'Oh, yes. They do sometimes.'
>
> 'Daddy?'
>
> 'Yes.'
>
> 'Where did Uncle George go?'
>
> 'He'll turn up all right.'
>
> 'Is dying hard, Daddy?'
>
> 'No, I think it's pretty easy, Nick. It all depends.'
>
> They were seated in the boat, Nick in the stern, his father rowing. The sun was coming up over the hills. A bass jumped, making a circle in the water. Nick trailed his hand in the water. It felt warm in the sharp chill of the morning.

From *Indian Camp* by Ernest Hemingway

It's easy to see how the short lines of the dialogue communicate the shock of the situation, and that the doctor doesn't feel like talking. But how does the writer continue this effect in the paragraph of description at the end? Study:

- The subject of each sentence.

- The structure of each sentence.

- The links between sentences.

- The visual images created.

In the next example, Billy is remembering the day his Dad left home after an evening at the cinema:

> The Big Picture. The End. Holding on to his dad's jacket in the crowd up the aisle and in the foyer. Then walking home, talking, questioning. Down the avenue. Then his dad not talking, not answering questions but hurrying. Billy running to keep up with him. What's a matter dad? What you running for? Uncle Mick's car outside. Jud inside it playing at the wheel. Stop here Billy. Jud driving like mad. His dad down the path, Billy after him, catching him through the kitchen door. Light flicking on in the living-room. His mother and Uncle Mick jumping up off the settee, staring and flushed. A trilby on the table. The flesh under his Uncle Mick's eye splitting as easily as a tangerine. The blood streaming out. Screaming. Shouting.

From *Kes* by Barry Hines

- Work out what actually happened.

- The story is told through Billy's eyes. Approximately how old was Billy and how do you know?

- In what ways is the style suited to Billy's age?

- How does the style communicate the emotion and drama of the event?

Try it

 Activity

- Now you try writing the next paragraph in which Billy's Dad packs his suitcase and leaves. Use the same style. You could look up the original scene at the end of *Kes*.

- Also try to write a short dialogue just after a guilty verdict has been delivered on someone who did not commit the crime. Write the exchange between the person and their parents, just before being taken down to the cell.

THE ART OF ANALYSIS:
Character study

Writers have many ways of painting a character:

- By comparison
- Evocative/revealing choice of words
- Use of descriptive detail
- Distinctive speech
- Emphasis, e.g. alliteration, repetition, contrast

- Revealing sentence structures
- Commenting directly

Consider how the character of Uncle is evoked in this extract:

I was staying at the time with my uncle and his wife. Although she was my aunt, I never thought of her as anything but the wife of my uncle, partly because he was so big and trumpeting and red-hairy and used to fill every inch of the hot little house like an old buffalo squeezed into an airing cupboard, and partly because she was so small and silk and quick and made no noise at all as she whisked about on padded paws, dusting the china dogs, feeding the buffalo, setting the mousetraps that never caught her; and once she sleeked out of the room, to squeak in a nook or nibble in a hay loft, you forgot she had ever been there.

But there he was, always, a steaming hulk of an uncle, his braces straining like hawsers, crammed behind the counter of the tiny shop at the front of the house, and breathing like a brass band, guzzling and blustery in the kitchen over his gutsy supper, too big for everything, except the great black boats of his boots. As he ate, the house grew smaller; he billowed out over the furniture, the loud check meadow of his waistcoat littered, as though after a picnic, with cigarette ends, peelings, cabbage stalks, birds' bones, gravy; and the forest fire of his hair crackled...

From *A Prospect of the Sea* by Dylan Thomas

By comparison _____
Buffalo
Brass band
Forest fire

Choice of words ⬭
Trumpeting, red-hairy, steaming, straining, crammed, guzzling, blustery, gutsy, billowed

---

Descriptive detail 〰
Fiery red hair
Boots like boats
Littered waistcoat

Emphasis ▭
Repeated references to size
Contrast with small wife
Alliteration: B

Sentence structures
Long sentences which pile up descriptive details

To write up your analysis, you must draw together all your points and stitch them together into a paragraph like this:

1 Start with a summarising sentence about the character.

2 Go through the methods used by the writer to present the character, mentioning the technique used, giving one or more examples, and then explaining how it creates an effect or impression.

3 End with an overview of the writer's skill or effect.

EXAMPLE

The presentation of Uncle is larger than life in every sense: he is a huge, impressive character who dominates the scene. The writer compares him to an old buffalo 'squeezed into an airing cupboard', 'a steaming hulk' with braces that 'strain like hawsers' like a huge, unstoppable animal. Telling verbs describe him as 'trumpeting', 'straining' and 'guzzling', and descriptive details of his straining braces, his littered waistcoat and fiery hair create an image of a man who is untidy and even uncontrollable. He does not fit, in any sense, behind the counter of the tiny shop. The writer repeats again and again the references to his huge size and the contrast with his small wife. Even the alliteration of 'b' in 'breathing like a brass band', 'black boats of his boots' and 'blustery' suggests his blundering movements. All these details are crammed into long sentences which extend to give more and more detail. The overall effect is one of unstoppable bulk. The writer has aimed to overwhelm the reader with his character, and succeeded.

Activity

Now try this yourself, focusing on the aunt. First use the prompts to point to examples of the writer forming an impression of the character.

Here is part of the extract again:

> I was staying at the time with my uncle and his wife. Although she was my aunt, I never thought of her as anything but the wife of my uncle, partly because she was so small and silk and quick and made no noise at all as she whisked about on padded paws, dusting the china dogs, feeding the buffalo, setting the mousetraps that never caught her; and once she sleeked out of the room, to squeak in a nook or nibble in a hay loft, you forgot she had ever been there.

Comparisons?

Choice of words?

Descriptive details?

Emphasis?

Sentence structure?

Next, write up your analysis using the sequence suggested, and borrowing from the style of the example.

MANAGING INFORMATION:
Research from scratch

Remind yourself of events so far in previous units.

If the wild child is David Brewster, then the British consul will consider whether the wolf boy should be returned to Britain. Carol decides to write an article exploring the issues that would be raised if such a decision were taken.

Carol hasn't thought this through before, and she doesn't know at this moment whether such a move would be legal, and what problems it might cause. She realises that she must first think through the possible issues and then make a list of all the things she needs to know and where she might start looking for the information.

1. Think through or talk through the issues

Make a list of issues raised by the prospect of bringing the wild child home to Britain. You have to cover all angles. The problem is, knowing what 'the angles' are.

You could do this by:

- Thinking about the problem from the point of view of different people, e.g. the boy himself, the consul, the Carpathian authorities, the remaining Brewster family. Put yourself in their shoes and imagine what they would think, ask and do.

- Thinking about the problem in chronological stages:

  - Getting approval to go.

  - Making the move.

  - Arriving in Britain.

  - First day or two in Britain.

  - First few months, etc.

- Thinking about the problem in terms of pros and cons, make two columns. Sometimes writing in one column will make you think of ideas for the other.

- Thinking of similar experiences or previous cases in the news, e.g. orphans brought to Britain.

- Playing out the events in your mind, as explained in Unit Seven.

2. Identify information you will need to collect

For each point you have listed, consider what further information is needed.

ISSUE	INFORMATION
Not yet sure he really is David Brewster	How to confirm his identity – blood test? – can the boy remember and how could we communicate to ask him?

3. Compile a list of research questions

Organise your questions helpfully under the people or places you will go to for information. In this way, when you speak to the consul, you will have a full list of questions ready.

Consul

Have the remaining Brewster family been approached about David if he returns?

What steps have been taken to establish the true identity of the boy?

Medical textbook or, as a back-up, a medical expert (who?)

What methods are available for confirming identity?

What would be involved in a blood test and how long would it take?

4. Plan the research

Suppose you, like Carol, have just 24 hours to conduct the research and write the piece. Draw a 24-hour timeline starting at noon and plan your research activities. Remember to sleep.

- Discuss the problems you are likely to encounter in researching an issue for which you need solid information.

- Under pressure of time, how do you decide what to pursue and what to leave?

SPELLING:
'OUS', 'EOUS' and 'IOUS'

These endings can be tricky because they share the same sound but not the same spelling.

Activity

With a partner, work out whether these words have an OUS, EOUS or IOUS ending:

mountain_____	spac_____	courag_____
gorg_____	simultan_____	relig_____
fur_____	griev_____	danger_____
outrag_____	marvell_____	ridicul_____
miscellan_____	flirtat_____	mischiev_____
spontan_____	consc_____	naus_____
var_____	dev_____	fam_____
hid_____	aqu_____	vic_____

Check your answers on page 136.

• What happens if the base word ends in soft 'G'?

• What happens if the base word ends in soft 'C'?

• What happens to complete words that end in a consonant, like MOUNTAIN?

• What happens when the root word ends with
   • E as in 'fame'?
   • F as in 'mischief'?
   • Y as in 'vary'?

• Which words *say* the 'E' in words ending 'EOUS'?

• Can you find any other patterns?

Activity

Change the following words by adding OUS, EOUS and IOUS endings. Remember that the base word might have to be altered.

glory	poison	advantage	melody
bulb	luxury	right	pomp
infect	joy	grace	envy

VOCABULARY:
Being concise

Look at this sentence:

Jamil had been left £10,000 by an unknown *person who supported him.*

If you knew the word 'benefactor', it could replace the four words at the end:

Jamil had been left £10,000 by an unknown *benefactor.*

Activity

With a partner, find a word to replace the phrases in boldface to make each of these sentences more concise:

1 The accident left Eleanor with a bone in her arm that had been **shifted out of position**.

2 My father was impressed by his **polite and considerate manner**.

3 All the work in the hostel for the homeless was performed by **people who gave their time and effort freely**.

4 The priest's **prediction of future events** left his community bewildered.

5 Enigma was a famous wartime **secret code that used letter substitutes**.

6 It had been distressing for the journalist who witnessed so many children suffering from **lack of food**.

7 The politician had **the special quality to inspire his followers with enthusiasm**.

8 I hate arguing with someone who remains **fixed in their opinions and ideas and cannot be persuaded to change**.

Check your answers on page 136.

Now go back to numbers 1, 3 and 6. Shorten these sentences even further without changing the meaning. You may need to rearrange the words.

READING BETWEEN THE LINES:
Exploring the imaginary world

Many stories are set in imaginary times and places. The fascination of these stories is the way the imaginary world is both similar to and different from our own.

Activity

Here is the unsettling opening of *Holes* by Louis Sachar. Read it looking for clues about when and where it is set, and how you realise it isn't an everyday place.

There is no lake at Camp Green Lake. There once was a very large lake here, the largest lake in Texas. That was over a hundred years ago. Now it is just a dry, flat wasteland.

There used to be a town of Green Lake as well. The town shriveled and dried up along with the lake, and the people who lived there.

During the summer the daytime temperature hovers around ninety-five degrees in the shade – if you can find any shade. There's not much shade in a big dry lake.

The only trees are two old oaks on the eastern edge of the "lake." A hammock is stretched between the two trees, and a log cabin stands behind that.

The campers are forbidden to lie in the hammock. It belongs to the Warden. The Warden owns the shade. Out on the lake, rattlesnakes and scorpions find shade under rocks and in the holes dug by the campers.

Here's a good rule to remember about rattlesnakes and scorpions: If you don't bother them, they won't bother you.

Usually.

Being bitten by a scorpion or even a rattlesnake is not the worst thing that can happen to you. You won't die.

Usually.

Sometimes a camper will try to be bitten by a scorpion, or even a small rattlesnake. Then he will get to spend a day or two recovering in his tent, instead of having to dig a hole out on the lake.

But you don't want to be bitten by a yellow-spotted lizard. That's the worst thing that can happen to you. You will die a slow and painful death.

Always.

If you get bitten by a yellow-spotted lizard, you might as well go into the shade of the oak trees and lie in the hammock.

There is nothing anyone can do to you anymore.

- The writer has set out to make the reader feel on familiar ground with ideas of a camp, a warden and a real place name. Pinpoint when and how the writer undermines your confidence in the familiar.

- Find one or two words which communicate the feel of the place, and pinpoint the details which gave you that impression.

- Turn to page 136 for more information about this book.

Activity

Creators of imaginary worlds invite readers into the imaginary world by treating them as though they already know the attitudes, customs and vocabulary of that world. The reader becomes a kind of tourist of this new world, soaking in the sights and sounds.

Here is part of the opening chapter of *Suth's Story* by Peter Dickinson.

They found their way without trouble. They were used to wide empty spaces, and their sense of direction was strong. Here and there they remembered the shape of a boulder, or a dry ravine, that they had passed on the outward journey. And the night dews freshened the faint scents that the Kin had left as they had come this way. There were no other smells to confuse them. Nothing lived here. In all the long day they had seen no tracks, nothing that moved, not a lizard, not even a scorpion. At least where there was nothing to eat there would be no big hunters stalking the night.

They walked at the steady pace that the Kin had used, journeying between one Good Place and the next. It grew colder. Slowly the moon rose. When it was almost halfway up the sky they stopped, without a word from either of them. They raised their heads and sniffed. Water.

'Moonhawk showed you this?' said Suth.

'No, not this. She showed me water in the hills.'

'We came by in the daytime. Why did we not smell this? Why did Bal not smell it? He finds water where no one else can find it.'

'I do not know. Is it a dew trap, Suth? Like the dew trap at Tarutu Rock?'

They turned and in a short while came to a wide pit in the ground. As they walked down into it they felt new layers of chill gathering around them. Soon the rocks they trod on were slippery with dew. But this was not like the dew trap they knew, where the moisture gathered at the bottom into a rocky pool, which didn't dry up until the sun was high. Here there was only a gravel floor and the water seeped away. They kneeled and licked the wetness from a large sloping boulder. It was not enough to swallow, but soothed their sore lips and parched mouths. For a little while they rested and licked and rested, then found their way back to their trail and walked on.

Identify clues that might help you to identify:

• The time and place.

• The characters, e.g. age, sex, background.

Identify where you are alerted to the fact that this world is different from anywhere today.

Turn to page 136 for more information about this book.

Write a paragraph in which a character is described making his or her way home, but weaving in a glimpse of a very different world in which your character lives.

IMPROVING SENTENCES:
Show stoppers

Sometimes writers use lines which are so striking that they stop the reader in their tracks. They attract attention to themselves because they are surprising, witty or funny in some very clever way. They make good openings, ends of chapters, high points and conclusions.

The ambush

Here is one from George Orwell:

> It was a bright cold day in April, and the clocks were striking thirteen.

From *1984* by George Orwell

This line is arresting because it starts off as an unremarkable factual sentence but there is a surprise lying in wait at the very last word. The reader is lulled into a false sense of security and ambushed by the impossible *thirteen*.

Activity

Conclude these sentence in a similar way, to spring a surprise on the reader.

It was twilight, and over the horizon rose…

It was a simple stew, containing fresh vegetable, wine and…

Try using this sentence structure yourself in two further sentences, borrowing the shape of the original and the surprise in the last word.

The proverb

Here is another sentence:

> Happy families are all alike; every unhappy family is unhappy in its own way.

From *Anna Karenina* by Leo Tolstoy

This sentence sounds like a proverb. It is the kind of sentence that makes the reader think. Its two halves are balanced: happy and unhappy. The second half of the sentence is the most interesting: there is something rather dull about people who are all alike.

Activity

Try completing these sentences in the same way, to give the feel of a proverb by balancing the first half with the second:

Summer days are all alike; Autumn brings…

Good readers enjoy books; great readers…

Try using this sentence structure yourself, in two further sentences.

Try it

Activity

Here are three more sentences. For each sentence:
1 Analyse the structure of the sentence and what makes it arresting.
2 Try imitating the structure in two sentences of your own.

Hale knew, before he had been in Brighton three hours, that they meant to murder him.

From *Brighton Rock* by Graham Greene

Polly Alter used to like men, but she didn't trust them any more, or have very much to do with them.

From *The Truth about Lorin Jones* by Alison Lurie

Fanny Peronett was dead.

From *An Unofficial Rose* by Iris Murdoch

NARRATIVE STYLE:
Sympathetic setting

Explanation

The setting is more than just a backdrop to the action. Writers use it to create atmosphere. Sometimes it reflects or symbolises the events of the story.

Example

The setting might include:

- The weather

- The landscape

- The time of day

- Surroundings such as a room

Here, Charles Dickens, in *Great Expectations*, paints a dismal picture of the depressing landscape in which the boy Pip lives:

Ours was the marsh country, down by the river, within, as the river wound, twenty miles of the sea. This _____ place overgrown with nettles was the churchyard; and that Philip Pirrip, and also Georgiana wife of the above, were dead and buried, and that the_____ flat _____ beyond the churchyard, intersected with dykes and mounds and gates, with _____ cattle feeding on it, was the marshes; and that the _____leaden line beyond, was the river; and that the distant _____ lair from which the wind was rushing, was the sea; and that the small bundles of _____ growing _____ of it all and beginning to _____, was Pip.

'Hold your noise!' cried a terrible voice, as a man started up from among the _____ at the side of the church porch. 'Keep still you little devil, or I'll cut your throat!'

- What words might Dickens have chosen to make sure the reader gained an impression of a dismal and depressing landscape?

- Make your choices and compare them with Dickens' original choices on page 136. What do you find striking about them?

- In what way does the landscape reflect the mood and events of the story?

- Find some other words, not deleted, which also contribute to this mood.

And where is the chill in the next passage?

> The long, draughty subterranean passage was chilly and dusty, and my candle flared and made the shadows cower and quiver. The echoes rang up and down the spiral staircase, and a shadow came sweeping up after me, and one fled before me into the darkness overhead. I came to the landing and stopped there for a moment, listening to a rustling that I fancied I heard; then, satisfied of the absolute silence, I pushed open the baize-covered door and stood in the corridor.

From *The Red Room* by H G Wells

- Find examples of details included to chill the reader.

- Where else have you come across this particular type of setting, and what sort of story can you expect?

Try it

Activity

Setting 1
The plot so far: A confrontation has been brewing between the man and wife for several chapters. The atmosphere is angry and tense. The day is hot and humid. A storm brews. Tempers fray.

- Write the paragraph or two leading up to the confrontation, using the weather to build up and symbolise the coming argument.

Setting 2
The plot so far: Ten years ago, Anne gave up her fiancé because she was persuaded he wasn't good enough for her. Now he is back and flirting with her cousins. Anne realises she still loves him.
- Write a paragraph just after they have all gone out to have fun, leaving Anne alone in the house, staring out of the window as the rain starts to fall. Write this paragraph in a way that suggests Anne's low spirits.

THE ART OF ANALYSIS:
Effective answers

You have learnt that effective answers:

- answer the question specifically

- avoid retelling the story

- explain opinions and interpretations

- justify every point

- try to make a number of points

- are guided by the number of marks available

- use telling quotations as evidence

- pay attention to the language and the writer.

Read the following extract from *Great Expectations*, in which Pip meets Miss Havisham for the first time.

In an arm-chair, with an elbow resting on the table and her head leaning on that hand, sat the strangest lady I have ever seen, or shall ever see.

She was dressed in rich materials – satins, and lace, and silks all of white. Her shoes were white. And she had a long white veil dependent from her hair, and she had bridal flowers in her hair, but her hair was white. Some bright jewels sparkled on her neck and on her hands, and some other jewels lay sparkling on the table. Dresses, less splendid than the dress she wore, and half-picked trunks were scattered about. She had not quite finished dressing, for she had but one shoe on – the other was on the table near her hand - her veil was but half arranged, her watch and chain were not put on, and some lace for her bosom lay with those trinkets, and with her handkerchief, and gloves, and some flowers, and a prayer book, all confusedly heaped about the looking-glass.

It was not in the first few moments that I saw these things, though I saw more of them in the first moments than might be supposed. But, I saw that everything within my view which ought to be white, had been white long ago, and had lost its lustre, and was faded and yellow. I saw that the bride within the bridal dress had withered like the dress, and like the flowers, and had no brightness left but the brightness of her sunken eyes. I saw that the dress had been put upon the rounded figure of a young woman, and that the figure upon which it now hung loose, had shrunk to skin and bone.

Activity

What is Pip's impression of Miss Havisham in this extract?
Here are three answers written by pupils:

Ruth's answer

In this passage, Pip meets Miss Havisham for the first time. Miss Havisham was dressed in white – including her shoes, veil and hair. She was wearing jewellery which sparkled. She had not quite finished dressing since she was only wearing one shoe. Everything seemed very messy and disorganised on her dressing table. Miss Havisham was actually an old lady and the dress didn't fit her now. All of the things which should have been white had faded.

- Ruth needs to improve her answer. Can you give her three pieces of advice?

Jake's answer

Pip's impression of Miss Havisham is that she is 'dressed in rich materials – satins, and lace, and silks – all of white. Her shoes were white. And she had a long white veil dependent from her hair, and she had bridal flowers in her hair, but her hair was white.' Pip sees that she might be quite wealthy because, 'some bright jewels sparkled on her neck and on her hands, and some other jewels lay sparkling on the table.' Pip is surprised that she has not finished dressing and is even more surprised when he realises that she is old and withered and must have been wearing the wedding dress since she was a young girl. 'But, I saw that everything within my view which ought to be white, had been white long ago, and had lost its lustre, and was faded and yellow. I saw that the bride within the bridal dress had withered like the dress, and like the flowers, and had no brightness left but the brightness of her sunken eyes.'

- Jake also needs to improve his answer. Can you give him three pieces of advice?

Hatim's answer

Pip's impression of Miss Havisham changes during the course of the passage. At first, his overall impression is that everything is white: 'all of white'. There is so much to take in at first that his impression of her is one of 'bright jewels' and 'splendid dresses' but he soon realises that she is not completely dressed, 'she had but one shoe on' and that other items of clothing were 'confusedly heaped about the looking-glass.' Gradually, Pip's impression changes as he realises that Miss Havisham is an old lady and he is shocked to realise that she must have been wearing these clothes since she had the 'figure of a young woman' many years before. Now, however, he is horrified to realise that the bride is 'faded', 'withered' and 'shrunk'.

- Hatim's teacher was pleased with this answer. What do you consider to be its strengths?

- Try writing a similar answer – perhaps as a group – to the question: What is Pip's impression of the room in this extract? Afterwards compare answers.

MANAGING INFORMATION: Editing down

Once you write up information, you become an information provider rather than a researcher. All published material is subject to constraints of space. Reporters try to write for the space they know they will have. Sometimes they have to add or delete material to make it fit.

On occasion, space is cut back radically because a big new story arrives which takes priority. The ability to edit back involves making choices about what is important, relevant and most interesting.

Opposite is a real article from *The Daily Mail* about a television documentary shown three weeks later: 'The Boy who lived with Monkeys'.

Task 1

Edit the article to retain the basic factual information: in other words, summarise the content of the article. You are not writing for an audience, so pay attention to the factual content. It must come out at one third of its current length. You do not need to write the article, but just do the deletions.

Summary

You can:

- Cut out the less important points.
- Cut out examples and illustrations.
- Cut out direct speech (you could report the gist of what was said in your own words).
- Generalise by rolling togther several similar points into one general point.
- Change words and stitch the remaining bits together.

Task 2

Edit the same article down a second time but on this occasion it will be published in the newspaper. You are writing in newspaper style for readers. Your choices will be different because the story must hold the reader's attention. Again, just mark the deletions; there is no need to write up the article.

Discuss:

- The difficulties of editing down to a particular length and how you make decisions.

- The practicalities of editing: what order you do it in, how you mark out the deletions, how you calculate the length.

- The difference between simply summarising and editing for a particular audience and purpose.

As a tribeswoman was scouring the forest clearing for firewood, she spotted a group of monkeys. Animated and chattering, they were a familiar enough sight to those who lived in the wilds of Uganda. But when the woman took a closer look, she could not believe her eyes. One member of the group was screaming just like the others and was unable to walk upright. But what she saw was unmistakably a human... a young boy. Astonished, the woman raced back to her village and summoned help.

Returning to the clearing in numbers, the villagers chased the naked youngster and cornered him up a tree. He was terrified of the strange humans confronting him and hurled sticks at them. The monkeys also made efforts to rescue him and had to be beaten back. Screaming and scratching, the boy was dragged from the tree and taken back to the Kamuzinda Christian Orphanage, 100 miles from the capital Kampala. He was unable to talk and in a terrible physical state, with wounds and scales covering his filthy body. To his clear disgust, he was washed and dressed.

That was eight years ago. It was the first step in a long and painstaking rehabilitation process that brought him back into the human fold. During that time a remarkable story has emerged, one that is the equal of any fanciful work of fiction.

Soon after the boy was found, a villager identified him as John Ssabunnya, who disappeared aged three. The boy's father had vanished after his mother was found murdered. It is believed that John was abandoned in the forest in 1988. He was discovered and adopted by a family of monkeys. He became one of them, picking up their sounds, mannerisms and eating habits and even learning to climb trees proficiently. For three years, he was fed by the animals on their diet of fruit, nuts and berries and treated like one of their own.

The fact he has been able to relate anything of this extraordinary part of his life is down to the efforts of Paul and Molly Wasswa who are responsible for 1,500 children at the orphan village. Over the months and years under their care, John was gradually taught to behave like a human. So successful has the transformation been that when John, now 14, arrives in Britain next month with a children's choir from his homeland, there will be nothing to distinguish him from the 19 other young singers in national costume.

But no-one should underestimate the huge leap that it has involved. Commenting on his arrival eight years ago, Mr Wasswa said: 'His actions and his way of living was that of the monkey. My own child Rachel was so frightened of him as I brought him into my house. I reminded her that underneath all of this was a small boy.'

John's father is said to have been traced and when he saw the state of his son, refused to take him in. Weeks later the father was killed in the civil unrest of the early Nineties.

Mr Wasswa continued: 'At first when we fed him he would take his food and pull it tight into his chest and retreat to a corner to eat. Slowly through much love and care the monkey boy became a miracle boy. One who now sings, laughs and plays like any other child.'

During the initial months back among humans John became ill and depressed refusing food and missing his monkey friends. But eventually he began to trust the people who cared for him and in time his shrieks were replaced by basic language. John was able to communicate to Mr Wasswa a little of how he lived with five monkeys – two of them young – and described how they would throw him their food as a game. Mr Wasswa added: 'We don't even know exactly how long he was in the forest. But I suspect he would have died of cold and wounds if he had not been rescued when he was.'

A BBC team from the Living Proof documentary series has investigated John's life. After extensive research the researchers are convinced of the story's authenticity. A spokesman said: 'For years and years there have been stories of feral children but they have had no scientific validity. In this case we think we have proven categorically the story is true.'

This page may be photocopied. By permission of *The Daily Mail*.

UNIT ONE
Spelling

definite, temperature, separate, pursue, miracle, compromise, vegetable, original, college, consonant, benefit, desperate, margarine, marriage, controversial, octagon.

UNIT TWO
Spelling

Fox – 3

Fish – 3

Duck – 3

Rabbit – 5

Cow – 2

Snake – 4

Vocabulary

ecology – environment

criminology – crime

meteorology – weather, atmosphere

astrology – possible effects of stars and planets

geology – earth's structure

technology – machines

ornithology – birds

psychology – human behaviour

theology – religion

etymology – the development of words

- Delete 'Y' and add 'IST' to create the name of the specialist. The exception is 'astrologer'.
- Delete 'Y' and add 'ICAL' to create an adjective.
- Delete 'Y' and add 'ICALLY' to create an adverb.

UNIT THREE
Spelling

appal, appalled, appalling;

acquit, acquitted, acquitting;

banquet, banqueted, banqueting;

batter, battered, battering;

prohibit, prohibited, prohibiting;

occur; occurred, occurring;

admit, admitted, admitting.

UNIT FOUR
Spelling

candle	parable	fizzle	
medical	shovel	critical	
cobble	grovel	travel	
edible	noticeable	signal	puddle

- Use 'LE' when the ending is preceded by double letters (but be aware of many exceptions, e.g. channel, funnel, tunnel).

- Use 'LE' if the ending is the suffix 'ABLE' or 'IBLE'.

- Use 'AL' if the word ends in hard 'C'.

- Use 'AL' if there is a recognisable base word, e.g. comic, magic, monument

- Use 'EL' if it can be heard rhyming with 'SELL'.

Improving sentences

If 'he said' comes **after** the speech:

- If the speech ends in a question mark or exclamation mark, that will do. It goes before the speech mark.

- If the speech ends in a full stop, the full stop converts to a comma. This also goes before the speech mark.

If 'he said' comes **before** the speech:

- put a comma before the speech mark

- start the speech with a capital letter as usual.

If 'he said' **interrupts** a sentence:

- put commas before and after the interruption, each before its speech mark

- start the speech with a capital letter as usual, but start the second half (after the interruption) with a small letter, so the reader can see that it is a continuation of the same sentence.

If 'he said' **interrupts between** sentences:

- put commas before and after the interruption, each before its speech mark (as above)

- re-open the speech with a capital letter so the reader can see it is a new sentence.

Narrative style

Original order: C, J, B, F, E, I, A, H, D, G.

The art of analysis

We went to the shop and bought sherbet and sucked it through sticks of liquorice. <u>Sucked</u> gently, the sherbet merely <u>dusted</u> the tongue; too hard, and you <u>choked</u> with sweet powders; or if you blew back through the tube the sherbet-bag burst and you <u>disappeared</u> in a blizzard of sugar. Sucking and <u>blowing</u>, coughing and <u>weeping</u>, we <u>scuffled</u> our way down the lane. We drank at the spring to clean our mouths, then <u>threw</u> water at each other and made rainbows. Mr Jones's pond was <u>bubbling</u> with life, and covered with great white lilies – they <u>poured</u> from their leaves like candle-fat, ran molten, then <u>cooled</u> on the water. Moorhens plopped, and dabchicks <u>scooted</u>, insects rowed and <u>skated</u>. New-hatched frogs hopped about like flies, lizards <u>gulped</u> in the grass. The lane itself was <u>crusted</u> with cow-dung, hard baked and smelling good.

UNIT SIX
Spelling

carpenter, particular, solicitor, occur, calculator, protester, farmer, undertaker, mortar, emperor, calibre, character, calendar, similar, teacher, gardener, peculiar, professor.

Improving sentences

Metaphorical verbs: lurched, sat frozen, juggled, squealing, wrenched, pinballing.

UNIT SEVEN
Reading between the lines

Last line:

> 'That's good,' said a little voice. 'Now we're safely locked in for the night.'

To brace the reader for a chilling conclusion:

- Creepy old-fashioned setting.

- It is night and dark.

- The girl is vulnerable being young and alone.

- We aren't told her name, so it feels slightly unreal.

- Repeated mentions of her security checks keep the reader's mind focused on her fear and the possible dangers.

- In the original, the story is called 'Boo!'.

To create a shock ending:

- The ending is short and sudden for maximum impact.

- The information that someone or something is in the room is withheld until the very last line.

- The use of direct speech makes the surprise character seem very real.

- The reader empathises with the girl's fear but doesn't really expect there to be any real threat to her – until the end.

- The identity of the 'little' voice is not revealed.

- All the sentences begin with 'She' except the last one: you know instantly that something has changed.

Narrative style

About the ending:

The girl has realised that she is a ghost. She lived in the house during her lifetime. If you read the first paragraph carefully, it also contains a possible clue about how she died. There are also a number of symbols of death and decay in the passage, e.g. the felled tree.

UNIT EIGHT
Spelling

persuasion	education	possession
magician	admission	detention
comprehension	satisfaction	musician
politician	production	explosion
mathematician	qualification	organisation
reputation	discussion	exception
rejection	permission	relation
potion	Russian	Prussian
extension	physician	promotion
consumption	percussion	emotion
corrosion	erosion	detention
inflation	commission	fiction

Most common: 'TION'

Unique to place names: 'SIAN'

Used on words ending in 'D' or 'S' sound: 'SION'

Used on words ending in 'T' sound: 'TION'

Used on words ending in 'MIT': 'SSION'

Use of words ending in 'IC': 'CIAN'

Sounds like 'ZH': 'SION'

Unusual example: ocean

Improving sentences

To introduce an example or illustration:
   for example
   such as
   for instance
   as revealed by
   in the case of

To qualify a point:
   however
   although
   unless
   except
   if
   as long as
   apart from
   yet

To add to or extend an idea:
   and
   also
   as well as
   moreover
   too

To contrast ideas:
   whereas
   instead of
   alternatively
   otherwise
   unlike
   on the other hand

To link cause and effect:
   because
   so
   therefore
   thus
   consequently
   as a result of

To emphasise a particular point:
   above all
   in particular
   especially
   significantly
   indeed
   notably

To compare ideas:
   equally
   in the same way
   similarly
   likewise
   as with
   like

UNIT TEN
Spelling

mountainous, spacious, courageous, gorgeous, simultaneous, religious, furious, grievous, dangerous, outrageous, marvellous, ridiculous, miscellaneous, flirtatious, mischievous, spontaneous, conscious, nauseous, various, devious, famous, hideous, aqueous, vicious.

Vocabulary

1 dislocated   5 cipher

2 courtesy   6 malnutrition

3 volunteers   7 charisma

4 prophecy   8 obstinate

Reading between the lines

Holes by Louis Sachar is set in a extreme punishment or 'boot' camp for young offenders in a future America. Both the environment and the treatment are harsh.

Suth's Story by Peter Dickinson is one of a series of books about The Kin, a migrating tribe of early *homo sapiens* living 200,000 years ago.

Narrative style

Dickens' original:

> Ours was the marsh country, down by the river, within, as the river wound, twenty miles of the sea. This <u>bleak</u> place overgrown with nettles was the churchyard; and that Philip Pirrip, and also Georgiana wife of the above, were dead and buried, and that the <u>dark</u> flat <u>wilderness</u> beyond the churchyard, intersected with dykes and mounds and gates, with <u>scattered</u> cattle feeding on it, was the marshes; and that the <u>low</u> leaden line beyond, was the river; and that the distant <u>savage</u> lair from which the wind was rushing, was the sea; and that the small bundle of <u>shivers</u> growing <u>afraid</u> of it all and beginning to cry, was Pip.
>
> 'Hold your noise!' cried a terrible voice, as a man started up from among the <u>graves</u> at the side of the church porch. 'Keep still you little devil, or I'll cut your throat!'